You Are The Gender You Are - Understanding Gender Identity

The Spectrum's Voice, Volume 2

AF Junior

Published by Spectrum Publishing, 2024.

While every precaution has been taken in the preparation of this book, the publisher assumes no responsibility for errors or omissions, or for damages resulting from the use of the information contained herein.

YOU ARE THE GENDER YOU ARE - UNDERSTANDING GENDER IDENTITY

First edition. April 18, 2024.

Copyright © 2024 AF Junior.

ISBN: 979-8224852727

Written by AF Junior.

Table of Contents

The book "*You Are The Gender That You Are*" is like a puzzle you didn't know you needed but are really glad you found. Each piece is a mix of facts and feelings that help you understand what makes you, well, you! Just like how every puzzle piece is unique, so is every person's gender identity. No two are the same, which makes it so unique.

The book takes a close look at how many different things affect who you feel you are on the inside. It's like sorting the edges and corners of a puzzle first. Some of those pieces are biological, like the hormones zooming around in your body or how your brain is wired. These aren't things you can pick and choose. They're just part of you.

But hey, a puzzle isn't just corners and edges, right? There are those middle pieces, too, that make the picture complete. In the same way, your psychological sense of self, how you feel and think, fills in those spaces. This book clarifies that how you see yourself is super personal and something only you can know.

Now, let's not forget the box the puzzle comes in! That's like the society you live in. The picture on the box kinda sets your expectations, doesn't it? Society often lays out roles and rules based on what it thinks a certain gender should be. Sometimes, that can mess with your puzzle-building, making you feel like you should fit in a certain way even when you don't. The book helps you see that it's cool to question those so-called rules.

If you're LGBTQIA+ and trying to make sense of growing up and figuring out who you are, this book is like your puzzle buddy. It won't put the pieces together, but it'll help you see where they might fit.

The Spectrum

"The Spectrum" serves as a unifying term for the LGBTQIA+ community, drawing inspiration from how visible light travels through a prism and separates into a beautiful rainbow of colors due to varying wavelengths. Rather than employing acronyms like LGBTQIA+ that compartmentalize the community into letters and subgroups, "The Spectrum" celebrates our uniqueness while acknowledging that we share similar struggles in our quest for societal acceptance and inclusion.

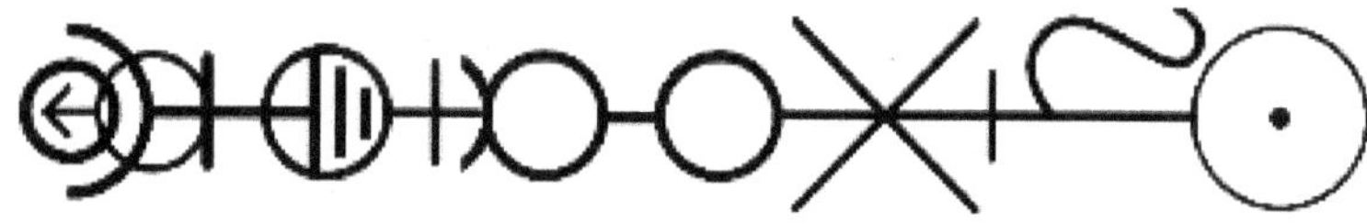

Lark Code

The LARK Code,, and others will do the same. it is like a secret recipe for feeling good about who you are, especially if you're part of the LGBTQIA+ community. Each letter stands for something important, and when you put them all together, they guide you on how to live your life positively. Let's break it down.

Love Yourself

"Love Yourself." This is the cornerstone, like the foundation of a building. If you don't have love for yourself, it's hard to build anything good on top of that. Loving yourself means giving yourself a break when you mess up and celebrating when you do well. It means caring for your body and mind because you know you're worth it.

"Love Yourself" isn't just a cool saying. It's the core of everything. Think of it like the roots of a tree. Without strong roots, the tree can't grow big and sturdy. Your love for yourself is like those roots, giving you the base you need to grow into the amazing person you're meant to be.

What does it mean to love yourself? Let's talk about mistakes. Everybody messes up. it's part of being human. Loving yourself means you don't beat yourself up over it. You say, "Okay, that happened. What can I learn?" instead of, "I can't believe I did that. I'm so stupid." It's like falling off a bike. You don't just lie there. you get up, dust off, and hop back on.

Celebrating your wins is another part of loving yourself. Did you get a good grade? Make a new friend? Figure out something important about your identity? That's awesome, and it's totally okay to be proud of it. Give yourself a mental high-five or even a little dance. Enjoying your achievements helps build up your confidence, like putting money in a happiness bank.

Taking care of your body and mind is crucial, too. Imagine your body's like a car. You wouldn't put the wrong fuel in it, right? Eating well, getting enough sleep, and exercising are all ways to love yourself because they keep your "car" running smoothly. Don't forget your mind, either. Activities like reading, meditating, or even just taking quiet moments to think can be like a spa day for your brain.

And hey, loving yourself isn't a one-and-done deal. It's an ongoing process, like keeping a garden. You have to water the plants, pull the weeds, and give them plenty of sunshine. The more you work on loving yourself, the more natural it becomes. Over time, you'll notice the strong foundation you've built, and you'll realize you're more ready than ever to tackle whatever comes next in your life.

Accept Yourself

Then comes "Accept Yourself." This is about saying yes to who you are deep down. Whether you're gay, straight, bi, trans, or still figuring it out, this is you saying, "This is me, and that's okay." Accepting yourself is like having an all-access pass to the best parts of life because you're not holding yourself back.

"Accept Yourself" is like the next level in a video game after "Love Yourself." Once you've got that base of self-love, accepting yourself is how you unlock new skills and powers. It's about looking in the mirror and saying, "Yep, that's me, and I'm good with it."

For starters, accepting yourself often means facing some truths. Maybe you realize you're gay, or bi, or trans, or non-binary. Or perhaps you're still figuring it out, like a puzzle you're putting together. That's all okay. The key is to not shove those pieces aside just because they don't fit what you thought they should be. You have to let the pieces of you be what they are, not what someone else says they should be.

Being honest with yourself like this is like turning on a light in a dark room. Suddenly, you can see where you're going and find things you didn't even know were there. This clarity helps you make better decisions, from the big stuff, like what job you want, to smaller things, like which people you want to spend time with.

But hey, accepting yourself isn't always easy. Sometimes, it's scary, like standing at the edge of a diving board for the first time. You might be afraid of what people will say or how things might change. It's natural to feel this way, but remember

holding back because of fear is like keeping that all-access pass in your pocket and never using it. You miss out on so many awesome experiences that way.

The cool thing about accepting yourself is that it's like giving yourself permission to be happy. You're saying, "I deserve to experience life as the real me, not someone I'm pretending to be." And once you take that step, it's like a whole new world opens up. You find new friends, new opportunities, and maybe even new sides of yourself you didn't know were there.

In the grand scheme of things, "Accept Yourself" is your ticket to a more authentic life. You get to explore, make mistakes, learn, and, most importantly, be you. And that's the best adventure of all.

Respect Yourself

"Respect Yourself" is the next piece. Imagine you're your own best friend. You wouldn't let people walk all over your best friend, right? The same goes for you. Respecting yourself means setting boundaries, standing up for what you believe in, and not letting anyone treat you badly.

"Respect Yourself" is like your personal shield and armor in the game of life. It helps you fend off things that could hurt you and lets the good stuff in. This is where you draw the lines, setting up your personal "no-go zones" that tell people how they can and can't treat you.

Let's dive into setting boundaries first. Imagine your life is like your bedroom. You wouldn't let just anyone come in, mess up your stuff, and leave, right? Setting boundaries is like putting a lock on your door. It means saying "no" when you need to and making sure you have space and time for yourself. Maybe that means telling a friend you can't hang out because you need a break or letting someone know that certain topics are off-limits for you. It's all about keeping your "room" neat and safe.

Now, standing up for what you believe in is like planting your flag on the ground. Say you see someone being bullied or hear a friend making a hurtful joke about the LGBTQIA+ community. Your gut tells you it's wrong. Respecting yourself means listening to that gut feeling and doing something about it, whether that's speaking up or getting help. Even if your voice shakes, that's your flag waving high, showing what you stand for.

But what about not letting anyone treat you badly? This is like having a strong castle wall around your kingdom. When people throw negative stuff your way—hurtful comments, stereotypes, or even just bad vibes—you don't let it in. You remember your worth, and don't let anyone chip away at it. If someone tries to, it's a sign that they shouldn't be inside your castle walls, so to speak.

Respecting yourself ties in closely with loving and accepting yourself. It's like a trilogy of books where each part makes the whole story richer and more exciting. When you respect yourself, it helps you love and accept yourself more because you're taking actions that reinforce your own values.

In short, "Respect Yourself" is like the code of honor for your personal kingdom. It's the rules and laws that keep things running smoothly, protect your treasures, and let you live your best life. And just like a wise and fair ruler, when you respect yourself, others are more likely to respect you, too.

Know Yourself

Finally, we have "Know Yourself." This is the detective work. It's about exploring your feelings, your likes and dislikes, and even your past to find clues about who you are. The better you know yourself, the easier it is to make choices that make you happy.

"Know Yourself" is like being a detective in the most exciting mystery ever—your own life. Imagine you have a magnifying glass, and you're searching for clues about who you really are. From the books you like to read to how you feel when you're alone is a clue.

Explore your feelings. Do you know those times when you're happy, sad, angry, or confused? Don't just brush those feelings aside. they're important clues. Ask yourself, "Why am I feeling this way?" Figuring out your emotions is like piecing together a puzzle. The more pieces you have, the clearer the overall picture becomes.

Let's talk about likes and dislikes. Say you love playing basketball but can't stand math class. That tells you something, right? Maybe you're more into physical activities and don't enjoy sitting at a desk. Or perhaps you like team sports but not working alone. These are like breadcrumbs leading you toward what makes you happy and what doesn't.

Don't forget to look into your past, too. It's like going through old photos and letters in your attic. You'll find clues about why you are the way you are today. Maybe you used to be super into art as a kid but gave it up. Why did you stop? Would picking it up again make you happy now? Your past can give you big hints about what you might enjoy in the present or future.

The awesome part is the more you know yourself, the easier it becomes to navigate life. Faced with a choice between two jobs? If you know you love working with people, that office job might not be for you. Do you have the option to join different clubs at school? If you know you're passionate about the environment, maybe the eco-club is your scene.

Knowing yourself also helps you stand up for yourself. If someone tries to push you into something you don't want, you'll be like, "Nope, I know that's not for me." It's your personal compass, always pointing you toward what's good for you.

"Know Yourself" isn't just a cool ending to the LARK Code. It's your toolkit, your map, and your compass all rolled into one. It's how you solve the mystery of you. And trust me, that's a mystery worth solving.

...And Others Will Do The Same.

Ah, the bonus level - "...and others will do the same." Think of it like a chain reaction, where one small move sets off a whole bunch of other moves. Or, like dropping a pebble in a pond—the ripples go out farther than you might expect.

When people see you loving, accepting, respecting, and knowing yourself, they pick up on it. It's like you're giving them permission to do the same for themselves. Plus, when you treat yourself well, people are more likely to treat you well in return.

When you're living the LARK Code, people notice. It's like you're glowing, and that light attracts others. Have you ever been around someone who just seems really comfortable with who they are? It feels good, right? It's like they're sending out a vibe that says, "It's cool to be yourself." By loving, accepting, respecting, and knowing yourself, you're sending out that same vibe. You're basically giving others the green light to start their own self-discovery journey.

This ripple effect doesn't just touch your friends and family. it can go way beyond that. Imagine you're in a classroom, and you stand up against a bully. The other kids see that and think, "Wow, if they can do it, maybe I can too." Or maybe you openly talk about your own experiences and challenges. Someone else who's been feeling the same way hears you and suddenly doesn't feel so alone. Your actions could be the nudge they needed to start loving, accepting, respecting, and knowing themselves, too.

Now, let's talk about how treating yourself well encourages others to treat you well. It's like setting the rules of a game. If you show that you won't accept bad behavior from yourself, others will think twice before treating you poorly. Respect attracts respect, like a magnet. And when people see you making choices that make you happy, they're more likely to support you in those choices. They'll think, "Hey, they really know what they're doing. I should respect that."

This bonus part isn't just a cherry on top. it's like the secret sauce that makes everything even better. By taking care of yourself, you're sending out ripples that can turn into waves of positive change. You're setting an example that can help others find their own path to happiness. And that's a win for everyone.

Putting It Together

Putting all these pieces together, the LARK Code becomes a sort of life map. It doesn't make the journey easy, but it gives you the tools to navigate it, kind of like having a compass, a first-aid kit, and many energy bars in your backpack. When the road gets tough, or you're not sure which way to go, you can look to LARK to find your way.

"The Man In The Arena"

"The Man in the Arena" is a famous passage from a speech given by Theodore Roosevelt, the 26th President of the United States. It's from his speech "Citizenship in a Republic," which was delivered at the Sorbonne in Paris, France, on April 23, 1910. The passage is notable because it emphasizes the value and honor of the individual who tries, regardless of success or failure, compared to those who criticize from the sidelines.

Here's The Passage

"It is not the critic who counts. not the man who points out how the strong man stumbles, or where the doer of deeds could have done them better. The credit belongs to the man who is actually in the arena, whose face is marred by dust and sweat and blood. who strives valiantly. who errs, who comes short again and again, because there is no effort without error and shortcoming. but who does actually strive to do the deeds. who knows great enthusiasms, the great devotions. who spends himself in a worthy cause. who at the best knows in the end the triumph of high achievement, and who at the worst, if he fails, at least fails while daring greatly, so that his place shall never be with those cold and timid souls who neither know victory nor defeat."

This quote has been cited frequently to inspire courage, effort, and persistence in the face of adversity. It serves as a reminder that it's far better to try and possibly fail than to avoid trying altogether for fear of failure.

The Man In The Arena, Paired With The Book

When paired with "You Are The Gender That You Are," the speech's themes can provide a powerful supplement to the book's core message. Here's how

Courage In Self-Discovery

Roosevelt emphasizes the importance of daring greatly, of being the person in the arena "whose face is marred by dust and sweat and blood." For many, coming to terms with one's own gender identity is an "arena" of its own, fraught with challenges but also ripe for self-discovery. It takes courage to challenge societal norms and question the gender one has been assigned at birth. This courage is also what the book encourages, telling its readers to be brave in exploring themselves.

Resilience In The Face Of Criticism

Both the speech and the book stress the significance of rising above societal judgments. Roosevelt mentions that the person who fails while daring greatly is far better than the person who never enters the arena. The book echoes this by highlighting the importance of loving, accepting, respecting, and knowing oneself despite societal pressures or criticisms.

The Worth Of Individual Experience

"The Man in the Arena" asserts that the value is in the doing, not in the outcome. Similarly, the book doesn't offer a one-size-fits-all answer but rather encourages each individual to go on their unique journey to discover their gender identity. Each person's "arena" is different, but what matters is the willingness to enter it and fight one's own battles.

The Complexity Of Life's Arena

Just as Roosevelt discusses how various qualities such as courage, intellect, and hard work contribute to the man in the arena's efforts, the book talks about how biological, psychological, and social factors all interact to shape one's gender identity. Life isn't simple, and neither is the journey to understanding oneself.

Empowerment

Both works ultimately aim to empower the individual. While Roosevelt focuses on the general virtues of courage and effort, "You Are The Gender That You Are" hones in on the self-empowerment found through understanding one's gender identity. The LARK Code can even be seen as a specific way to apply Roosevelt's broader advice to the particular challenges and joys of exploring one's gender.

YOU ARE THE GENDER YOU ARE - UNDERSTANDING GENDER IDENTITY

"The Man in the Arena" can serve as a philosophical backbone for the real-life, practical advice given in "You Are The Gender That You Are." While Roosevelt's speech encourages courage and resilience in any challenging endeavor, the book provides the specific tools and understanding needed for the complex journey of discovering one's gender identity. Both tell us that the struggle itself is a worthy one, deserving of respect and full engagement.

A Puzzle Box With No Picture On The Cover

12

YOU ARE THE GENDER YOU ARE - UNDERSTANDING GENDER IDENTITY

Imagine stumbling upon a puzzle box with no picture on the cover. Intriguing, right? You're not entirely sure what the final image will be, but you're excited to dive in and find out. That's the kind of journey the book "You Are The Gender That You Are" offers. Just like that mysterious puzzle, this book helps you explore the complex and deeply personal world of gender identity without forcing you into a predetermined picture. It's not just a how-to guide or a list of definitions. it's more like a map that highlights various routes you can take to understand yourself better.

Now, why is a book like this so important, especially for the LGBTQIA+ community? Think about how confusing and overwhelming it can be to sort through all those puzzle pieces without a guide. This book acts as a kind-hearted friend who not only has done a few puzzles before but also respects that your puzzle—your gender identity—is yours and yours alone to put together. It's an invitation to explore, understand, and eventually embrace your authentic self.

One of the best parts about this book is how it covers a lot of ground. Just like a puzzle has edge pieces, middle pieces, and those weirdly shaped ones that you're not sure where to place, this book discusses the biological, psychological, and social factors that contribute to your gender identity. It digs deep into how your brain structure, hormone levels, feelings, and the society you live in all work together in this intricate dance that makes you who you are.

Plus, this book doesn't shy away from the societal rules and roles that often act like the picture on the puzzle box—limiting and sometimes misleading. It helps you see that it's perfectly fine to challenge these expectations and, even better, to redefine them. It's like saying, "Hey, who needs a box cover? Your puzzle, your rules."

It all starts with The Lark Code. Love yourself, Accept yourself, Respect yourself, and Know yourself. Think of these as the corner pieces that hold your puzzle together. They're the foundation that supports you as you navigate the winding and sometimes confusing paths of gender identity.

If you're looking to figure out what makes you tick or simply want to understand the vast diversity of human experience better, "You Are The Gender That You Are" is like the puzzle buddy you never knew you needed. It won't solve the puzzle for you, but it'll hand you the pieces one by one, letting you discover how they fit together to create the unique masterpiece that is you.

Importance Of Understanding And Accepting

Understanding and accepting one's own gender identity is like finding the core puzzle piece that helps the rest of the puzzle make sense. It's that central, and that's why it's so important. If you're shaky on that piece, you might feel lost or like something's off, but you can't put your finger on it.

Let's talk biology. Imagine your body's like a computer with pre-installed software. This "software," like hormones and brain structure, affects how you experience gender. When you understand how your "system" is built, it can make you feel more at home in your own body.

Then there's the psychological part. This is the "you" in your head, your self-image, and your feelings. Being cool with your gender identity helps you feel more solid here. It's like knowing the rules of a game. Once you understand them, you can play better and even bend them to make the game your own.

Don't forget about society and culture. They're like the outer circle of friends who chime in with their opinions, wanted or not. These voices often come with a list of dos and don'ts based on gender. Understanding your own identity helps you figure out which social rules fit you and which don't. It's like picking which advice to listen to and which to ignore.

Being cool with your own gender identity isn't just good for you. it's good for everyone around you. When you're confident about who you are, it helps others feel okay to be themselves, too. It spreads good vibes, like how one lit sparkler can light up a bunch more.

When you get to know your own gender identity, you're not just learning about a label or a category. You're learning about yourself—what makes you happy, what makes you feel safe, and what makes you feel most like yourself. That's like finding those really tricky pieces of the puzzle that you've been searching for. they make everything else click into place.

And don't forget, puzzles are more fun when you're not stressed about making a mistake. If you're comfortable with your gender identity, you're more likely to be comfortable in your own skin. You can interact with people and face challenges without that nagging worry about whether you're being your "real" self. It's like having the box lid with the finished picture right next to you. it guides you.

Now, what about other people? Well, when you understand and accept yourself, it's easier for others to do the same. Your friends and family can see the whole completed puzzle and appreciate it for what it is—a unique and amazing work of art, which is you!

Plus, there's a ripple effect. The more people see that it's cool to be yourself, the easier it becomes for everyone else to be themselves. It's like when you finish a puzzle and want to show it off. Others see it and think, "Hey, maybe I can do that puzzle too!"

Yeah, getting to know and accept your own gender identity? It's more than important—it's essential. It's the key to understanding yourself, which is the first step in living a life where you can be happy, loved, and free to be you. Grasping your own gender identity is a huge part of knowing who you are. When you get it, it's like finally finding your place in a big, complicated puzzle. And once that happens, you can focus on other awesome stuff, like chasing your dreams and building strong friendships.

Embracing Diversity And Uniqueness

Embracing diversity and uniqueness within the LGBTQIA+ community is like working on one of those mega puzzles with thousands of pieces, where each piece is completely different but super important for the big picture. You might have pieces that are all sorts of shapes, sizes, and colors, and guess what? You need every single one to make the puzzle complete.

In the LGBTQIA+ community, there's a rainbow of experiences, identities, and backgrounds. Some people might identify as gay, others as transgender, and still others as non-binary, asexual, or queer. Just like how some puzzle pieces have straight edges, and some have wavy ones, people in the community are diverse and unique in their own ways.

Now, why is this a big deal? Well, for starters, when everyone is different but still part of the same puzzle, it makes for a more interesting and complete picture. If every piece looked the same, the puzzle would be pretty boring, right? The same goes for a community. Different perspectives and experiences make the group more vibrant.

Another cool thing is that when you embrace diversity, you learn a lot, not just about others but about yourself. It's like when you're stuck on a hard section of the puzzle, and someone else shows you a different way to approach it. You pick up new ideas and strategies that you might not have thought of on your own.

But it's not just about making the community better. It's about making the world better, too. When people outside the LGBTQIA+ community see how diverse and unified it can be, they start to get it. They see that being different is not just okay. It's awesome. That can help knock down stereotypes and change attitudes, making the world a safer, happier place for everyone.

And let's not forget embracing diversity also means standing up for each other. In a puzzle, each piece has its place and value. If one is missing or damaged, it affects the whole thing. Similarly, supporting the unique identities within the LGBTQIA+ community means standing against discrimination and inequality. It sends a strong message.

Every piece of the puzzle is important and deserves respect.

Embracing diversity and uniqueness within the LGBTQIA+ community is kinda like building the most epic, colorful, and amazing puzzle ever. And the best part? When everyone's included, the puzzle isn't just complete. it's a masterpiece.

Should There Be Standards?

Should there be standards, guidelines, or etiquette the LGBTQIA+ community follows to be oneself and still be part of society to not be bullied?

In an ideal world, everyone should be free to be themselves without fear of bullying or discrimination, regardless of their sexual orientation, gender identity, or any other characteristic. However, society often has norms and expectations, some of which can be restrictive.

While some people advocate for guidelines or etiquette within the LGBTQIA+ community to navigate societal expectations, it's important to note that these shouldn't be about conforming to make others comfortable at the expense of one's own identity. Instead, the focus should be on fostering respect and understanding both within and outside of the community.

Education and Awareness

One of the most effective ways to combat ignorance and prejudice is through education. People within the LGBTQIA+ community can help educate others about different identities and experiences, which can create a more accepting environment.

Mutual Respect

Whether it's respecting someone's pronouns or their choices in how they express their gender or sexuality, respect is a two-way street. Respecting others' boundaries while asserting one's own can be a balancing act but is crucial for everyone's well-being.

Safe Spaces

Creating and maintaining environments where people can freely express their identities can be incredibly empowering. Whether it's an online forum or a physical space like an LGBTQIA+ center, safe spaces give people the freedom to be themselves without judgment.

Standing Up Against Bullying

Suppose they see bullying or discriminatory behavior, whether online or in person. In that case, they can choose to intervene if it's safe to do so or support the victim in whatever way they can.

Unity And Support

Sometimes, the greatest strength comes in numbers. Being there for one another, sharing experiences, and offering emotional support can make a world of difference for someone who is struggling.

Legal Rights

Knowing one's legal rights when it comes to discrimination can be empowering. Armed with this knowledge, they can better stand up for themselves and others in various settings, like the workplace or healthcare facilities.

Self-Care

This is an individual responsibility as much as it is a communal one. They can't be their best selves in society if they're not taking care of their mental, emotional, and physical health.

Be Yourself

This is the most important point. The only standard or guideline anyone should really follow is to be true to themselves. Conforming to someone else's idea of what is acceptable can lead to a loss of personal identity and self-worth.

It's a tricky balance to maintain, but the ultimate goal should be a society where guidelines are not necessary because acceptance and respect are given freely to all, regardless of their gender or sexual orientation.

What is Gender Identity?

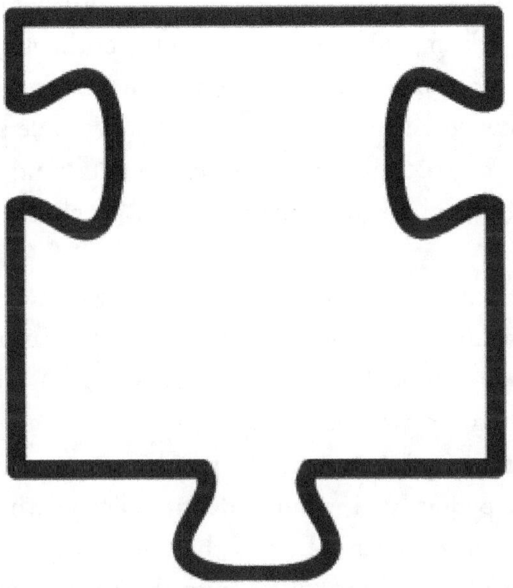

Gender Identity

Gender identity is like a puzzle piece that fits into who you are. It's the deeply-held sense of being male, female, a blend of both, or neither. It's not just about the body you're born with or the clothes you wear, but it's about how you feel inside and how you express yourself. Just like a puzzle piece, your gender identity is unique to you and may take time to understand and accept. It's all about finding the piece that feels right for you, no matter what anyone else thinks.

Imagine your gender identity as the central piece of a complex puzzle that makes up who you are as a person. This puzzle includes various aspects of your identity, such as your thoughts, feelings, experiences, and how you perceive yourself in relation to the world around you.

Your gender identity is like a specific puzzle piece that fits into this larger picture. For some people, their gender identity aligns with the sex they were assigned at birth (male or female), and they may identify as cisgender. For others, their gender identity may differ from their assigned sex, leading them to identify as transgender, nonbinary, genderqueer, or another gender identity that resonates with them.

Understanding your gender identity involves exploring and recognizing your innermost feelings and sense of self. It's about discovering which puzzle piece feels most authentic to who you are, regardless of societal expectations or norms. This process can be deeply personal and may evolve over time as you learn more about yourself and your identity.

Some folks know their gender identity from a super young age. Like, a boy might feel that he's really a girl inside, even if everyone else says he's a boy. Others might take a bit more time to figure it out, especially with all the noise from society saying how they "should" be.

Here's the thing

figuring out one's gender identity is kind of like putting together a puzzle. Different pieces like feelings, experiences, and even dreams help form a complete picture. And nobody else can complete that puzzle for them—it's a personal journey.

It's also crucial to note that gender identity can be fluid. That means it might change over time, and that's okay! It doesn't make it any less real or important. Some people might start out thinking they're a guy but later realize they're non-binary, which means they don't feel strictly male or female. Others might identify as genderqueer, genderfluid, or a whole bunch of other terms that resonate with them.

The key takeaway is that gender identity isn't a one-time decision or something that can be seen on an X-ray. It's an ongoing process of self-discovery that belongs to each individual. It's a critical part of their identity, like a fingerprint—unique to them and them alone. And however they identify, it's valid and deserves respect.

In The Lgbtqia+ Community

In the LGBTQIA+ community, where diversity in gender identity is celebrated and embraced, this perspective is particularly empowering. It encourages individuals to explore and honor their true selves, free from the constraints of conventional gender norms.

Imagine stepping into a community where every puzzle piece is not only accepted but celebrated for its uniqueness. Here, the focus is not on fitting into pre-established categories dictated by society but rather on constructing a self-identity that resonates with one's deepest sense of being. It's like entering a room filled with puzzles of all shapes, sizes, and colors, where each puzzle is valued for its individuality and contribution to the collective mosaic of identities.

In this inclusive space, individuals are encouraged to embrace their authentic selves and express their gender identity in ways that feel most genuine to them. Whether someone identifies as transgender, nonbinary, genderqueer, or any other gender identity, they are supported in their journey of self-discovery and self-expression.

Rather than adhering to rigid gender norms that dictate how one should look, behave, or identify, members of the LGBTQIA+ community are empowered to challenge and redefine these norms. They are encouraged to explore the full spectrum of gender expression and to embrace the fluidity and complexity of their identities.

Within this supportive community, individuals find strength in solidarity, knowing that they are not alone in their journey. They have access to resources, support networks, and spaces where they can connect with others who share similar experiences and identities.

Moreover, by celebrating diversity in gender identity, the LGBTQIA+ community fosters a culture of acceptance, understanding, and respect for all individuals, regardless of their gender identity or expression. It's about creating a world where everyone is free to be their authentic selves without fear of judgment or discrimination.

In essence, the LGBTQIA+ community serves as a beacon of empowerment and liberation for individuals exploring their gender identity. It's a place where people can boldly embrace their true selves, knowing that they are accepted, valued, and celebrated for who they are.

Distinction Between Gender Identity And Biological Sex

A lot of people think gender identity and biological sex are the same thing, but they're really not. They're related, sure, but they're two different concepts.

Imagine gender identity and biological sex as two distinct puzzle pieces that, while interconnected, each contributes to the larger picture of who you are. Biological sex refers to the physical attributes you are born with, such as chromosomes, hormones, and reproductive anatomy. It's like one piece of the puzzle that helps define your physical characteristics.

On the other hand, gender identity is the deeply-held sense of being male, female, a blend of both, or neither. It's not determined solely by your biology but rather by how you perceive yourself and identify internally. This puzzle piece represents your innermost feelings, thoughts, and sense of self in relation to gender.

While biological sex and gender identity may align for some people, they can also diverge for others. For example, a person assigned female at birth based on their anatomy may identify as male, while another person assigned male at birth may identify as nonbinary. These experiences highlight the distinction between biological sex and gender identity and emphasize that one does not necessarily dictate the other.

Understanding the difference between gender identity and biological sex is crucial for promoting inclusivity and affirming the experiences of transgender and nonbinary individuals. It acknowledges that gender is not solely determined by physical characteristics but rather by a complex interplay of biological, social, and psychological factors.

By recognizing the unique puzzle pieces that make up each person's identity, we can foster a more inclusive and understanding society where everyone is respected and valued for who they are, regardless of their gender identity or biological sex. It's about embracing the diversity of human experience and celebrating the myriad ways in which individuals define and express their gender.

Biological Sex

Biological sex is what a doctor announces when someone is born, based on physical characteristics like genitals and reproductive anatomy. It's also influenced by chromosomes, those tiny structures found in every cell of the body that carry genes and determine various biological traits. Typically, people are classified as male or female at birth based on these physical attributes.

When A Baby Is Born

When a baby is born, it's a moment filled with anticipation and excitement. Still, it's also a time when societal norms and expectations come into play. One of the first things that happens is the doctor or healthcare provider makes a quick assessment of the baby's external genitalia to determine their sex designation. This initial classification is often recorded on the birth certificate, becoming an integral part of the individual's official identity from the very beginning of their life journey.

For most people, this assigned sex designation aligns with their internal sense of gender identity—the deeply felt sense of being male, female, a blend of both, or neither. From early childhood, individuals are socialized and treated according to the sex they were assigned at birth. They're given names, pronouns, and societal roles that correspond to this designation, shaping their experiences and interactions with the world around them.

For many individuals, this alignment between assigned sex and internal gender identity feels natural and affirming. It's like finding the missing puzzle piece that fits seamlessly into the larger picture of who they are. Their external appearance and societal expectations align with their internal sense of self, providing a sense of congruence and validation.

However, it's essential to recognize that this alignment isn't universal. For some individuals, the sex assigned at birth may not accurately reflect their true gender identity. This disconnect between assigned sex and internal gender identity can lead to feelings of confusion, distress, and dysphoria.

Transgender and nonbinary individuals, for example, may experience a discrepancy between their assigned sex and their deeply felt sense of gender. They may identify as a gender different from the one they were assigned at birth or may reject traditional gender categories altogether. For these individuals, embracing and affirming their true gender identity often involves a journey of self-discovery, self-acceptance, and, in some cases, gender-affirming medical interventions.

Understanding and respecting the diversity of gender identities is crucial for creating inclusive and supportive environments where all individuals can thrive. It's about recognizing that everyone deserves the right to define and express their gender in a way that feels authentic to who they are, regardless of societal expectations or norms.

Spectrum With A Myriad Of Possibilities

Biological sex, often thought of as a clear-cut concept, actually exists along a spectrum with a myriad of possibilities. While the majority of individuals are classified as either male or female at birth based on typical biological traits, it's crucial to acknowledge that not everyone fits neatly into these categories. Enter intersex variations – a testament to the rich diversity of human biology.

Intersex individuals are born with biological traits that don't conform to the traditional definitions of male or female. These variations can manifest in a variety of ways, challenging our preconceived notions of what it means to be male or female. Some intersex individuals may have differences in their external genitalia, such as an enlarged clitoris or an underdeveloped penis. Others may have variations in their internal reproductive organs, such as having both ovarian and testicular tissue or a combination of both male and female reproductive structures.

Additionally, intersex variations can extend to chromosomes, the genetic blueprints that play a fundamental role in determining biological sex. While the majority of individuals have either XX (female) or XY (male) chromosomes, intersex individuals may have variations such as XXY, XO, or other combinations. These chromosomal differences can have a profound impact on an individual's development. They may influence their physical characteristics and reproductive abilities.

Understanding and respecting intersex variations is essential for promoting inclusivity and affirming the experiences of intersex individuals. It's about recognizing that biological sex is not always straightforward or binary and that diversity is a natural and beautiful part of the human experience.

By raising awareness about intersex variations and advocating for the rights and dignity of intersex people, we can create a more inclusive and understanding society where everyone's experiences and identities are recognized and respected. It's about embracing the complexity and diversity of human biology and celebrating the unique qualities that make each individual who they are.

Chromosomes

Imagine your body as a complex puzzle, with each piece playing a crucial role in how it functions. In this puzzle, chromosomes are like the instruction manual, neatly tucked away inside every single cell. They hold the key to many aspects of your biological makeup.

Now, most people have either XX chromosomes or XY chromosomes. If you have XX chromosomes, it typically indicates that you're biologically female, while XY chromosomes often mean you're biologically male. It's like being assigned a certain piece in the puzzle, dictating some of your physical characteristics and traits.

But here's where it gets interesting

biology doesn't always follow the simple XX or XY pattern. Sometimes, the puzzle pieces can be a bit different. For example, some people have XXY chromosomes or XYY chromosomes, or even other unique combinations. It's like finding unexpected pieces that don't quite fit the usual categories, adding complexity and diversity to the puzzle of human biology.

XX Chromosomes

XX chromosomes are a pair of sex chromosomes found in the majority of individuals who are biologically female. These chromosomes serve as a blueprint, containing genetic instructions crucial for various aspects of development and functioning within the female body.

In the intricate puzzle of human biology, XX chromosomes represent a significant piece, guiding the formation of female characteristics. They carry a wealth of genetic information encoded in their structure, including genes responsible for traits such as reproductive processes, hormone regulation, and physical features specific to females.

During the process of reproduction, when an egg (or ovum) from a female is fertilized by a sperm from a male, the resulting embryo typically inherits one X chromosome from each parent, resulting in an XX chromosome pair in females. This genetic composition sets the foundation for the development of female reproductive organs, such as the ovaries and uterus, as well as the manifestation of secondary sexual characteristics like breast development and wider hips during puberty.

Beyond reproductive functions, XX chromosomes also play a role in influencing various aspects of health and well-being throughout a person's life. They contribute to the regulation of hormonal balance, immune system function, and susceptibility to certain genetic disorders that may be linked to genes located on the X chromosome.

While XX chromosomes are commonly associated with individuals who identify as female, it's important to recognize that biological sex and gender identity are not always perfectly aligned. Some individuals with XX chromosomes may identify as male, female, or non-binary, highlighting the complex interplay between biology, identity, and individual experience. In essence, XX chromosomes represent a foundational element in understanding the diverse tapestry of human biology and identity.

XY Chromosomes

XY chromosomes are a pair of sex chromosomes typically found in individuals who are biologically male. These chromosomes serve as a blueprint, containing genetic instructions crucial for various aspects of development and functioning within the male body.

In the intricate puzzle of human biology, XY chromosomes represent a significant piece, guiding the formation of male characteristics. They carry a wealth of genetic information encoded in their structure, including genes responsible for traits such as reproductive processes, hormone regulation, and physical features specific to males.

During the process of reproduction, when a sperm from a male fertilizes an egg (or ovum) from a female, the resulting embryo typically inherits one X chromosome from the mother and one Y chromosome from the father, resulting in an XY chromosome pair in males. This genetic composition sets the foundation for the development of male reproductive organs, such as the testes and penis, as well as the manifestation of secondary sexual characteristics like facial hair and deeper voice during puberty.

Beyond reproductive functions, XY chromosomes also play a role in influencing various aspects of health and well-being throughout a person's life. They contribute to the regulation of hormonal balance, immune system function, and susceptibility to certain genetic disorders that may be linked to genes located on the X or Y chromosome.

While XY chromosomes are commonly associated with individuals who identify as male, it's important to recognize that biological sex and gender identity are not always perfectly aligned. Some individuals with XY chromosomes may identify as female, male, or non-binary, highlighting the complex interplay between biology, identity, and individual experience. In essence, XY chromosomes represent a foundational element in understanding the diverse tapestry of human biology and identity.

XXY Chromosomes And XYY Chromosomes

XXY chromosomes and XYY chromosomes are variations of sex chromosome compositions that differ from the typical XX and XY pairs found in most individuals.

XXY chromosomes, also known as Klinefelter syndrome, occur when a male has an extra X chromosome, resulting in a total of 47 chromosomes instead of the usual 46. This additional X chromosome can lead to a variety of physical and developmental differences. Individuals with XXY chromosomes often have characteristics such as reduced fertility, increased height, and differences in sexual development compared to typically developing males. They may also experience challenges related to hormone levels and sexual maturation. However, with appropriate medical care and support, individuals with XXY chromosomes can lead fulfilling lives.

XYY chromosomes, on the other hand, involve an extra Y chromosome in males, resulting in a total of 47 chromosomes. This condition, known as XYY syndrome, is typically associated with increased height and a slightly higher risk of certain behavioral and developmental differences. However, many individuals with XYY chromosomes lead healthy and productive lives. Not all may exhibit noticeable physical or cognitive differences.

In the puzzle of human genetics, XXY and XYY chromosomes represent unique pieces that deviate from the standard XX and XY patterns. These variations highlight the complexity and diversity of human biology, showing that individuals can have different chromosomal compositions that influence their physical and developmental traits. Understanding these variations is essential for providing appropriate support and care to individuals with XXY or XYY chromosomes, emphasizing the importance of acceptance and inclusivity in our understanding of human diversity.

Intersex

Intersex is a term used to describe individuals who are born with variations in sex characteristics that do not fit typical definitions of male or female. These variations can involve chromosomes, gonads, sex hormones, or genitalia. They may manifest in a wide range of physical and biological differences.

In the puzzle of human biology, intersex individuals represent a unique piece that challenges traditional notions of binary sex. While biological sex is often thought of as strictly male or female, intersex variations highlight the complexity and diversity of human anatomy and genetics.

Intersex variations can occur for various reasons, including genetic factors, hormonal imbalances during fetal development, or differences in the sensitivity of cells to sex hormones. Some common intersex variations include differences in genitalia development, such as ambiguous genitalia or a combination of male and female genital features. Others may involve chromosomal variations, such as XXY (Klinefelter syndrome) or XO (Turner syndrome), or differences in gonadal development, such as having both ovarian and testicular tissue.

It's important to note that being intersex is not a medical condition or disorder but rather a natural variation of human biology. Intersex individuals are as healthy and capable as anyone else, and they have the right to self-determination and bodily autonomy.

However, intersex individuals may face challenges related to stigma, discrimination, and lack of understanding in society. This can include issues such as non-consensual medical interventions to "normalize" their bodies, as well as societal pressure to conform to binary notions of sex and gender.

Understanding and respecting the diversity of intersex experiences is essential for promoting inclusivity, dignity, and human rights for all individuals, regardless of their sex characteristics. By acknowledging and affirming the existence of intersex variation, we can work towards creating a more compassionate and inclusive society for everyone.

Hormones

What Are Hormones

Hormones are vital chemical messengers in the human body that regulate various physiological processes, including growth, metabolism, reproduction, and mood. They act as signaling molecules, traveling through the bloodstream to target cells and tissues, where they exert their effects by binding to specific receptors.

In the intricate puzzle of human biology, hormones play a central role in coordinating and controlling the body's growth and functions. Imagine them as the conductors of an orchestra, orchestrating the complex symphony of bodily processes to maintain balance and harmony.

Hormones are produced by specialized glands known as endocrine glands, such as the pituitary gland, thyroid gland, adrenal glands, and gonads (testes in males and ovaries in females), as well as by other tissues and organs. Each hormone has specific functions and targets, influencing various aspects of physiology and behavior.

For example, insulin, produced by the pancreas, helps regulate blood sugar levels by promoting the uptake of glucose into cells. Thyroid hormones, produced by the thyroid gland, control metabolism and energy expenditure. Estrogen and testosterone, produced by the ovaries and testes, respectively, play crucial roles in sexual development, reproduction, and secondary sexual characteristics.

Hormonal balance is essential for overall health and well-being. Imbalances in hormone levels can lead to a wide range of health issues, including metabolic disorders, reproductive disorders, mood disorders, and growth abnormalities.

Throughout life, hormone levels fluctuate in response to factors such as age, stress, nutrition, sleep, and environmental cues. Puberty, pregnancy, and menopause are periods of significant hormonal changes that can have profound effects on physical and emotional health.

Understanding the role of hormones in the body is essential for maintaining health and addressing hormonal imbalances or disorders. Medical interventions such as hormone replacement therapy (HRT) can help restore hormonal balance in conditions such as hypothyroidism, menopausal symptoms, or hormonal deficiencies.

In essence, hormones serve as the intricate communication system that regulates the body's growth, development, and functions, ensuring that each piece of the biological puzzle fits together seamlessly to support overall health and vitality.

Male Hormones

Male hormones, also known as androgens, are a group of hormones primarily produced in the testes and adrenal glands of males. The most well-known male hormone is testosterone, although other androgens contribute to male physiology as well.

YOU ARE THE GENDER YOU ARE - UNDERSTANDING GENDER IDENTITY

In the puzzle of human biology, male hormones are like master artisans, shaping many aspects of male development and functioning. They play a crucial role in the development of male reproductive organs during fetal development and puberty, as well as in the maintenance of male secondary sexual characteristics throughout life.

Testosterone, the primary male hormone, is responsible for promoting the development of male reproductive structures such as the testes and prostate gland. It also stimulates the production of sperm and supports male fertility. During puberty, testosterone triggers the growth of facial and body hair, deepens the voice, and promotes muscle growth and bone density.

In addition to testosterone, other androgens such as dihydrotestosterone (DHT) and androstenedione also contribute to male characteristics and functions. DHT, in particular, plays a role in the development of male secondary sexual characteristics such as facial hair growth and male pattern baldness.

Male hormones influence not only physical traits but also have significant effects on behavior, mood, and cognition. Testosterone, for example, is associated with traits such as aggression, competitiveness, and libido. However, it's important to note that the relationship between hormones and behavior is complex and influenced by many factors, including genetics, environment, and individual differences.

While male hormones are primarily associated with males, they also play important roles in females, albeit in smaller quantities. Females produce testosterone and other androgens in the ovaries and adrenal glands, contributing to aspects of female physiology such as libido, bone health, and muscle mass.

Maintaining hormonal balance is essential for overall health and well-being in both males and females. Imbalances in male hormones can lead to a variety of health issues, including infertility, erectile dysfunction, decreased libido, and mood disturbances.

Understanding the role of male hormones in the body is crucial for promoting optimal health and addressing hormonal imbalances or disorders that may arise. By recognizing the intricate interplay between hormones and various aspects of male physiology and behavior, we gain a deeper understanding of the complex puzzle of human biology.

Testosterone

Testosterone is a vital hormone primarily produced in the testes of males and in smaller amounts in the ovaries of females and the adrenal glands in both sexes. It belongs to a group of hormones called androgens. It plays numerous essential roles in the body, influencing both physiological and behavioral processes.

Development Of Male Reproductive Organs

During fetal development, testosterone is crucial for the formation and differentiation of male reproductive organs such as the testes, penis, and prostate gland. It directs the development of these structures, ensuring that they function properly later in life.

Secondary Sexual Characteristics

Testosterone is responsible for the development of secondary sexual characteristics in males during puberty. This includes the growth of facial and body hair, deepening of the voice, and increased muscle mass and bone density. These changes help distinguish males from females and play a role in sexual attraction and mate selection.

Sperm Production

Testosterone stimulates the production of sperm cells (spermatogenesis) in the testes. It is essential for maintaining male fertility and reproductive function. Adequate levels of testosterone are necessary for the normal development and maturation of sperm cells.

Libido And Sexual Function

Testosterone plays a significant role in regulating libido (sex drive) and sexual function in both men and women. It influences arousal, sexual desire, and the ability to achieve and maintain erections in males. In females, testosterone contributes to sexual arousal and the sensitivity of erogenous zones.

Muscle Growth And Strength

Testosterone is an anabolic hormone, meaning it promotes the growth and repair of muscle tissue. It stimulates protein synthesis in muscle cells, leading to increased muscle mass and strength. This is why testosterone is often associated with traits like athleticism and physical prowess.

Bone Health

Testosterone plays a role in maintaining bone density and strength. It helps regulate bone turnover by stimulating bone formation and inhibiting bone resorption. Adequate levels of testosterone are important for preventing conditions like osteoporosis and reducing the risk of fractures.

Mood And Cognitive Function

Testosterone can influence mood, cognitive function, and overall well-being. Low levels of testosterone have been associated with symptoms such as fatigue, irritability, and decreased motivation. Testosterone replacement therapy has been shown to improve mood and cognitive function in some individuals with low testosterone levels.

Overall, testosterone is a crucial hormone with diverse effects on the body. It not only plays a key role in male reproductive health and sexual function but also influences muscle mass, bone density, mood, and cognitive function. Maintaining optimal testosterone levels is important for overall health and well-being in both men and women.

Female Hormones

Female hormones refer to a group of hormones primarily produced in the ovaries, adrenal glands, and placenta (during pregnancy) of individuals assigned female at birth. These hormones, including estrogen and progesterone, play critical roles in regulating various physiological processes associated with female reproductive health, as well as influencing aspects of metabolism, mood, and bone density.

In the intricate puzzle of human biology, female hormones act as the architects, shaping the development and functioning of the female reproductive system and contributing to overall health and well-being. They orchestrate the menstrual cycle, support fertility, and play key roles during pregnancy and childbirth.

Estrogen is one of the primary female hormones. It is responsible for promoting the development of female reproductive organs, such as the uterus, fallopian tubes, and vagina. It also regulates the menstrual cycle, including the growth and shedding of the uterine lining. It influences secondary sexual characteristics such as breast development and body fat distribution.

Progesterone is another important female hormone, particularly during the menstrual cycle and pregnancy. It helps prepare the uterine lining for the implantation of a fertilized egg. It supports early pregnancy by maintaining the uterine environment. During the menstrual cycle, progesterone levels rise after ovulation to prepare the body for potential pregnancy and decline if pregnancy does not occur, leading to menstruation.

Other female hormones, such as follicle-stimulating hormone (FSH) and luteinizing hormone (LH), play crucial roles in regulating ovarian function and the menstrual cycle. FSH stimulates the growth and maturation of ovarian follicles. At the same time, LH triggers ovulation and the release of an egg from the ovary.

Beyond reproductive functions, female hormones also influence other aspects of health and well-being. Estrogen, for example, plays a role in maintaining bone density, cardiovascular health, and cognitive function. Progesterone may also have mood-stabilizing effects and contribute to overall emotional well-being.

Throughout a woman's life, hormonal levels fluctuate in response to factors such as age, stress, pregnancy, and menopause. Hormonal imbalances or disorders can lead to a variety of health issues, including irregular menstrual cycles, infertility, mood disturbances, and menopausal symptoms.

Understanding the role of female hormones in the body is essential for promoting women's health and well-being at every stage of life. By recognizing the intricate interplay between hormones and various aspects of female physiology and reproductive health, we gain a deeper understanding of the complex puzzle of human biology.

Estrogen

Estrogen is a group of hormones primarily produced in the ovaries in females, with smaller amounts produced in the adrenal glands and fat cells. These hormones play essential roles in regulating various physiological processes throughout the body, influencing reproductive health, sexual development, and overall well-being.

Female Reproductive System Development

Estrogen is crucial for the development and functioning of the female reproductive system. During fetal development, estrogen contributes to the formation of the uterus, fallopian tubes, and vagina. It also promotes the development of secondary sexual characteristics such as breast development and the distribution of body fat.

Menstrual Cycle Regulation

Estrogen plays a central role in regulating the menstrual cycle. It stimulates the growth and thickening of the uterine lining (endometrium) during the first half of the menstrual cycle, preparing it for the potential implantation of a fertilized egg. Estrogen levels fluctuate throughout the menstrual cycle, reaching their peak just before ovulation.

Ovulation

Estrogen levels rise sharply just before ovulation, triggering the release of an egg from the ovary. This surge in estrogen is essential for the maturation and release of the egg, making it available for fertilization by sperm.

Bone Health

Estrogen helps maintain bone density and strength by promoting bone formation and inhibiting bone resorption. It plays a crucial role in preventing bone loss and reducing the risk of osteoporosis, particularly in postmenopausal women.

Cardiovascular Health

Estrogen has protective effects on the cardiovascular system. It helps regulate cholesterol levels, promotes the dilation of blood vessels, and reduces inflammation, all of which contribute to cardiovascular health. Estrogen may also play a role in reducing the risk of heart disease in premenopausal women.

Mood And Cognitive Function

Estrogen influences mood, cognitive function, and overall well-being. Changes in estrogen levels, such as those experienced during the menstrual cycle, pregnancy, or menopause, can affect mood and cognitive function. Estrogen therapy has been shown to improve mood and cognitive function in some women, particularly those experiencing menopausal symptoms.

Vaginal Health

Estrogen helps maintain the health and elasticity of the vaginal tissues. It stimulates the production of vaginal lubrication and maintains the thickness of the vaginal lining, which is important for sexual function and comfort.

Overall, estrogen is a multifaceted hormone with diverse effects on the body. It plays a central role in female reproductive health, menstrual cycle regulation, bone health, cardiovascular health, mood, and cognitive function. Maintaining optimal estrogen levels is essential for overall health and well-being in women throughout their lives.

Know The Difference

Why is it important to know the difference? Well, because sticking to just biological sex can make things confusing and difficult for people whose inner feelings don't match their bodies. Imagine being forced to wear a shoe that doesn't fit just because it looks like it should. Ouch, right?.

YOU ARE THE GENDER YOU ARE - UNDERSTANDING GENDER IDENTITY

You know how sometimes you're working on a puzzle, and you find a piece that looks like it should fit, but when you try to jam it in, it just doesn't work? That's kinda like when people rely only on biological sex to understand someone's gender. Sure, the puzzle piece may look right at a quick glance, but it's not the perfect fit you need for the bigger picture.

See, just focusing on biology is like looking at a puzzle piece's shape but ignoring its colors and patterns. It's just part of the story. People are more than just what they look like on the outside or what their biology says they should be. There's a whole range of feelings, experiences, and yes, even science stuff like psychology that makes someone feel like a boy, a girl, neither, or both.

Imagine trying to walk around in shoes that pinch your toes and blister your heels just because someone else thinks they're the right fit for you. Sounds pretty miserable, huh? The same goes for sticking to just biological definitions of gender. It might make some folks really uncomfortable and even hurt inside.

knowing the difference between biological sex and gender identity helps everyone get a fuller picture of what makes people, well, people. And that's super important, especially for folks in the LGBTQIA+ community who are trying to figure out who they are while growing up. Understanding this difference helps to break down some walls and lets people express themselves in a way that feels right to them.

Because, hey, you wouldn't force a puzzle piece into a spot it doesn't belong, would you? The same goes for people and their feelings about their gender.

Respect For Identity

Recognizing the distinction between biological sex and gender allows us to respect and affirm individuals' identities as they define them. For many people, their gender identity may not align with the sex they were assigned at birth. By acknowledging and validating their self-identified gender, we show respect for their autonomy and self-expression.

Validation Of Gender Diversity

Understanding that gender is not strictly binary (male or female) but exists on a spectrum helps validate the experiences of transgender, nonbinary, and gender-nonconforming individuals. It acknowledges that there are many ways to experience and express gender beyond traditional notions of masculinity and femininity.

Promotion Of Inclusivity And Diversity

Embracing the diversity of gender identities fosters a more inclusive and equitable society where everyone feels valued and respected. It encourages us to challenge stereotypes and norms that limit individuals' self-expression and opportunities based on their assigned sex at birth.

Reduction Of Stigma And Discrimination

Misunderstanding or conflating biological sex with gender can perpetuate stigma and discrimination against transgender and gender-diverse individuals. It can lead to marginalization, harassment, and violence directed at those who do not conform to societal expectations of gender. By promoting understanding and acceptance of diverse gender identities, we can work to reduce stigma and discrimination in our communities.

Support For Mental Health And Well-Being

For individuals whose gender identity does not align with their assigned sex at birth, being forced to conform to societal expectations can lead to feelings of dysphoria, anxiety, and depression. Understanding and validating their gender identity can provide crucial support for their mental health and well-being, affirming their sense of self and reducing the negative impact of societal stigma and discrimination.

Advancement Of Human Rights

Recognizing the difference between biological sex and gender is essential for advancing human rights and social justice for all individuals, regardless of their gender identity or expression. It calls for legal protections against discrimination based on gender identity. It ensures access to healthcare, education, and employment opportunities for transgender and gender-diverse individuals.

Access To Healthcare

Understanding the difference between biological sex and gender is crucial for providing inclusive and appropriate healthcare services. Healthcare providers need to recognize and respect individuals' self-identified gender to provide effective and affirming care, particularly for transgender and gender-diverse patients. This includes access to gender-affirming treatments and procedures that align with individuals' gender identities.

Legal Recognition And Documentation

Distinguishing between biological sex and gender is necessary for ensuring legal recognition and documentation of individuals' gender identities. Many countries and jurisdictions now allow individuals to update their legal documents, such as identification cards, passports, and birth certificates, to reflect their self-identified gender. Legal recognition of gender identity is essential for protecting individuals' rights and preventing discrimination in various aspects of life, including employment, housing, and education.

Education And Awareness

Understanding the difference between biological sex and gender is essential for promoting education and awareness about gender diversity and inclusivity. By incorporating discussions of gender identity and expression into school curricula and public awareness campaigns, we can help combat stereotypes, prejudice, and discrimination based on gender. Education about gender diversity fosters empathy, understanding, and acceptance, creating more supportive and inclusive communities for all individuals.

Intersectionality

Recognizing the distinction between biological sex and gender allows us to understand the intersectionality of gender with other aspects of identity, such as race, ethnicity, sexual orientation, disability, and socioeconomic status. Intersectional approaches to gender acknowledge that individuals' experiences of gender are shaped by multiple intersecting factors and power dynamics. This understanding is essential for addressing the unique challenges and barriers faced by marginalized and intersectional communities within the broader context of gender equality and social justice.

Promotion Of Self-Acceptance And Empowerment

Understanding the difference between biological sex and gender promotes self-acceptance and empowerment for individuals who may struggle with their gender identity or expression. It encourages individuals to explore and embrace their authentic selves, free from the constraints of societal expectations or norms. By affirming diverse gender identities and expressions, we empower individuals to live authentically and confidently, contributing to their overall well-being and happiness.

Fostering Allyship And Advocacy

Distinguishing between biological sex and gender is essential for fostering allyship and advocacy for transgender and gender-diverse communities. Allies play a crucial role in advocating for the rights and dignity of transgender and gender-nonconforming individuals, challenging discrimination, and promoting social change. Understanding the nuances of gender identity and expression helps allies become effective advocates and allies in the fight for gender equality and inclusivity.

Understanding the difference between biological sex and gender is fundamental for promoting dignity, equality, and respect for all individuals. It requires us to acknowledge and affirm diverse gender identities and experiences, recognizing that everyone deserves the right to live authentically and free from discrimination. Just as forcing someone to wear ill-fitting shoes can cause discomfort and pain, denying someone the recognition of their gender identity can have profound and harmful consequences.

Societal Influence

Society Angle

Then there's the social angle. Society loves labels and categories, right? From the moment someone is born, they're often placed into a box marked "boy" or "girl." This comes with many "rules" about how to behave, what to wear, and even what hobbies to have. These social norms can make figuring out one's true gender identity a bit tricky because of all the noise and expectations.

Society's inclination towards categorization starts at birth, with individuals typically being assigned a gender based on physical anatomy. This assignment often comes with a predefined set of expectations and norms, which can profoundly influence an individual's understanding and expression of their gender identity.

These societal norms encompass a wide range of aspects, from behavior and appearance to interests and career choices. For instance, traditional expectations might dictate that boys are "supposed" to be assertive, interested in sports, and avoid showing vulnerability. At the same time, girls are often expected to be nurturing, interested in more domestic or artistic activities, and display emotional openness. Clothing and appearance also fall under these norms, with specific styles and colors traditionally associated with each gender.

These societal "rules" can create a considerable amount of noise and confusion for individuals exploring their gender identity. When a person's internal sense of gender does not align with the expectations associated with their assigned gender at birth, it can lead to a conflict between their true self and the role they feel pressured to perform. This dissonance can make the journey of self-discovery and acceptance challenging, as individuals must navigate through layers of societal conditioning to uncover their authentic identity.

For someone questioning or exploring their gender identity, these societal boxes can feel restrictive and invalidating. The pressure to conform to traditional gender norms can lead to feelings of alienation and confusion, particularly for those whose gender identity falls outside the binary categories of male and female.

In the context of the LGBTQIA+ community, the impact of these societal norms is particularly evident. Members of this community often face the challenge of reconciling their true gender identity with societal expectations. This journey requires not only personal courage and self-exploration but also navigating a social landscape that may not always be accepting or understanding.

The effort to dismantle these rigid societal norms and promote a more inclusive understanding of gender is an ongoing challenge. It involves advocating for a broader recognition of the diversity of gender identities and expressions and creating spaces where individuals can explore and express their true selves without the constraints of traditional gender boxes.

Societal norms and labels play a crucial role in shaping and sometimes complicating the exploration of gender identity. These norms often create a predefined framework that individuals are expected to fit into, which can clash with their internal sense of self. Navigating this landscape requires both personal resilience and a societal shift towards greater inclusivity and acceptance of gender diversity.

Society's Expectations

Society's expectations can feel like someone imposing rigid rules on a puzzle you're assembling, insisting that certain pieces must fit only in specific places because that's the way it's always been done. These expectations often come with labels and roles attached, dictating how individuals should look, behave, and identify based on perceived norms of what is considered "normal" or "right."

Just like when you're diligently putting together a puzzle, it can be frustrating and disheartening when society imposes limitations and constraints on people's identities and experiences. It's as if someone has disrupted the flow of your puzzle-building process by misplacing a crucial piece, making it difficult to achieve the picture you envision.

For example, society might expect individuals to conform to traditional gender roles, prescribing certain behaviors and characteristics based on assigned sex at birth. This can create pressure for individuals who don't fit neatly into these categories, leading to feelings of alienation, confusion, and self-doubt.

Similarly, societal expectations around career choices, relationships, and personal aspirations can limit people's potential and prevent them from fully expressing themselves. Just as you might struggle to find the right puzzle piece when someone has disrupted your flow, individuals may struggle to find their place in a society that insists on rigid conformity.

Breaking free from society's expectations requires courage, self-awareness, and resilience. It means challenging outdated norms and embracing diversity, recognizing that every individual is unique and deserves to be valued for who they are, not who others expect them to be.

Ultimately, society is like a vast puzzle with countless pieces, each contributing to the richness and diversity of the whole. By embracing differences, celebrating individuality, and rejecting narrow-minded expectations, we can create a more inclusive and compassionate world where everyone's puzzle can come together in their own unique way.

Gender Roles

Society's expectations regarding gender roles are like predetermined shapes in a puzzle, where individuals are pressured to fit into specific molds based on their perceived gender identity. These expectations dictate how people should behave, dress, and interact with others, often reinforcing traditional stereotypes and norms.

For example, society often expects men to be strong, assertive, and emotionally stoic. In contrast, women are often expected to be nurturing, caring, and emotionally expressive. These rigid gender roles can limit individuals' self-expression and opportunities for personal growth, as they may feel compelled to conform to societal expectations rather than explore their own interests and passions.

Moreover, these expectations can perpetuate inequalities and injustices, as they often prioritize certain traits or behaviors associated with one gender over another. For instance, men may be discouraged from pursuing careers in caregiving or the arts. At the same time, women may face barriers in male-dominated fields such as science, technology, engineering, and mathematics (STEM).

Furthermore, society's expectations of gender roles can also have harmful effects on individuals' mental health and well-being. Those who do not conform to traditional gender norms may face stigma, discrimination, and ostracization, leading to feelings of alienation, shame, and low self-esteem.

Breaking free from society's expectations of gender roles requires challenging these norms and advocating for greater gender equality and inclusivity. It involves recognizing that gender is a spectrum and that individuals should be free to express themselves in ways that feel authentic to them, regardless of societal expectations.

By promoting diversity, acceptance, and respect for all gender identities, we can create a more equitable and inclusive society where individuals are empowered to embrace their true selves and pursue their dreams without fear of judgment or discrimination. Just as each puzzle piece contributes to the beauty of the whole picture, every individual's unique expression of gender adds richness and diversity to the fabric of society.

Male Gender Roles

Male gender roles are societal expectations and norms that dictate how men should behave, think, and express themselves based on their perceived gender identity. These roles often reinforce traditional stereotypes and ideals of masculinity, shaping how men are expected to interact with others and navigate the world around them.

One aspect of male gender roles is the expectation of strength and stoicism. Men are often taught to suppress emotions such as vulnerability, sadness, and fear. Instead, exhibit traits like independence, resilience, and toughness. This can create pressure for men to appear confident and unshakeable, even in the face of adversity, leading to a reluctance to seek help or express their feelings openly.

Another common expectation is related to career and success. Men are often encouraged to prioritize their careers and financial success, equating their worth with their professional achievements and ability to provide for themselves and their families. This pressure to excel in the workplace can contribute to stress, burnout, and work-life imbalance for men.

Additionally, traditional male gender roles often emphasize dominance and aggression. Men may feel pressure to assert their authority and control in social and professional settings while also adhering to norms of competitiveness and toughness. This can lead to conflict and aggression, both within interpersonal relationships and in broader societal contexts.

Furthermore, there are expectations around physical appearance and athleticism. Men are often encouraged to conform to ideals of muscularity and physical fitness while also downplaying traits or interests that are perceived as feminine or non-conforming. This pressure to conform to a certain physical ideal can contribute to body image issues and unhealthy behaviors such as disordered eating and excessive exercise.

Challenging and expanding upon traditional male gender roles involves promoting a more inclusive and nuanced understanding of masculinity. It means recognizing that men, like all individuals, are diverse and multifaceted, with a range of interests, emotions, and experiences. Encouraging men to embrace vulnerability, empathy, and emotional expression can lead to healthier relationships and greater overall well-being.

Moreover, breaking free from rigid gender norms benefits not only men but society as a whole. By dismantling stereotypes and promoting gender equality, we create space for individuals of all genders to thrive and contribute fully to their communities. Ultimately, redefining male gender roles involves empowering men to embrace their authentic selves and live with integrity, compassion, and authenticity.

Female Gender Roles

Female gender roles are societal expectations and norms that dictate how women should behave, think, and present themselves based on their perceived gender identity. These roles are deeply ingrained in cultural beliefs and historical traditions, shaping women's experiences and opportunities in various aspects of life.

One prominent aspect of female gender roles is the expectation of nurturing and caretaking. Women are often socialized to prioritize the needs of others over their own and to excel in roles related to caregiving, such as parenting, homemaking, and emotional support. This can create pressure for women to fulfill traditional roles as wives, mothers, and caregivers, often at the expense of their personal ambitions and desires.

Additionally, there is often an emphasis on appearance and beauty standards for women. Society places value on physical attractiveness and adherence to certain beauty ideals, such as being thin, youthful, and conventionally attractive. This pressure to conform to narrow beauty standards can lead to body image issues, low self-esteem, and unhealthy behaviors such as disordered eating and cosmetic surgery.

Furthermore, traditional female gender roles often involve expectations around passivity and submissiveness. Women may be encouraged to be polite, accommodating, and deferential in their interactions with others while also downplaying assertiveness and ambition. This can limit women's opportunities for leadership and advancement in various domains, including the workplace and politics.

Another aspect of female gender roles is the expectation of domesticity and homemaking. Women are often expected to excel in roles related to housekeeping, cooking, and caregiving, regardless of their career aspirations or personal interests. This can create barriers for women who seek to pursue non-traditional paths or who aspire to achieve success outside of the home.

Challenging and expanding upon traditional female gender roles involves promoting a more inclusive and equitable society where women are free to pursue their passions and aspirations without limitations or constraints. It means recognizing and valuing the diverse contributions that women make to their families, communities, and society as a whole.

Empowering women to assert their agency, autonomy, and voice is essential for dismantling gender stereotypes and promoting gender equality. By challenging rigid gender norms and advocating for social change, we can create a world where women are free to define their own identities and roles without being confined by outdated expectations or limitations. Ultimately, redefining female gender roles involves creating space for women to thrive as whole individuals, with the freedom to pursue their dreams and fulfill their potential.

Pesky People

Navigating societal expectations can feel like assembling a puzzle. At the same time, pesky people hover over your shoulder, eager to dictate where each piece should go. These individuals, whether friends, family, or authority figures like teachers, often have their own preconceived notions of how you should fit into the puzzle of life based on their own experiences and beliefs.

Sometimes, these well-meaning individuals can provide valuable insights or support, acting as guiding lights in your puzzle-building journey. They might offer advice, share their wisdom, or provide a missing piece you didn't even realize you needed. Their encouragement and guidance can help you navigate challenges and overcome obstacles, bringing clarity and direction to your puzzle.

However, there are also times when these same individuals may try to impose their own expectations onto your puzzle, insisting that certain pieces should fit into specific spots regardless of whether they truly belong there. This can lead to confusion, frustration, and even feelings of hurt or inadequacy.

For example, a family member might pressure you to pursue a career path that aligns with their own aspirations, ignoring your unique interests and talents. Or a friend might criticize aspects of your identity or lifestyle that don't conform to their idea of what is "normal" or "acceptable." In these instances, the pressure to conform to others' expectations can feel suffocating, stifling your ability to authentically express yourself and find your own place in the puzzle of life.

Learning to assert your own agency and autonomy is essential for navigating these challenges. It means recognizing that you are the architect of your own puzzle, with the power to choose which pieces to include and where they belong. While the input of others can be valuable, ultimately, you are the one who knows yourself best and has the right to define your own path.

In the end, building your life puzzle is a journey of self-discovery and empowerment. Embracing your individuality, trusting your instincts, and staying true to your authentic self are essential ingredients for creating a puzzle that reflects who you truly are and brings you joy and fulfillment.

Setting Boundaries

Setting boundaries and asserting your own needs and desires are crucial steps in protecting your puzzle from unwanted interference and manipulation. Here's how

Identify Your Needs and Desires

Take time to reflect on what matters most to you and what you need to feel fulfilled and happy. This might include identifying your values, passions, and goals for the future. By understanding your own needs and desires, you can better advocate for yourself and communicate your boundaries to others.

Communicate Clearly

Once you've identified your needs and desires, it's important to communicate them clearly and assertively to those around you. Be direct and specific about what you're comfortable with and what you're not. Don't be afraid to express yourself honestly, even if it means setting boundaries that others may not agree with.

Set Healthy Boundaries

Boundaries are limits that you set to protect your physical, emotional, and mental well-being. These boundaries can take many forms, from saying no to requests that feel overwhelming or draining to establishing limits on how others can treat you or speak to you. Setting boundaries is not about being selfish or rude. It's about prioritizing your own needs and self-care.

Enforce Boundaries Consistently

Once you've established boundaries, it's important to enforce them consistently. This means holding firm to your boundaries even when others push back or try to test them. Remember that you have the right to say no and to protect your own well-being, even if it means disappointing or upsetting others.

Surround Yourself with Supportive People

Building a strong support network of friends, family, and mentors who respect and celebrate your uniqueness is essential for personal growth and self-discovery. Surround yourself with people who uplift and encourage you and who appreciate you for who you are, flaws and all. These supportive relationships can provide a safe and nurturing environment for you to thrive and pursue your goals.

Practice Self-Care

Taking care of yourself physically, emotionally, and mentally is essential for maintaining healthy boundaries and protecting your well-being. Make time for activities that bring you joy and relaxation, and prioritize self-care practices such as exercise, mindfulness, and spending time with loved ones.

By setting boundaries and asserting your own needs and desires, you can create a safe and empowering environment for personal growth and self-discovery. Surrounding yourself with supportive individuals who respect and celebrate your uniqueness will help you navigate life's challenges with confidence and resilience.

Religious Expectations

Religious expectations of gender roles often stem from interpretations of religious texts, cultural traditions, and historical practices within religious communities. These expectations dictate how individuals should behave, interact, and fulfill their roles based on their perceived gender identity within the context of their faith.

Traditional Gender Roles

Many religious traditions uphold traditional gender roles that emphasize distinct responsibilities and expectations for men and women. For example, within some religious communities, men may be expected to assume leadership roles in the family and community. At the same time, women are often relegated to domestic duties and caregiving roles. These roles are often justified through interpretations of religious texts and teachings that prescribe specific gender roles and behaviors.

Modesty And Dress Codes

Religious expectations of gender roles often include guidelines for modesty and dress codes, particularly for women. Modesty standards may vary widely among different religious traditions. Still, they often dictate how individuals should dress and present themselves in public spaces. This can include requirements for women to cover their hair, wear modest clothing, and adhere to specific dress codes to maintain their perceived purity and modesty.

Marriage And Family Roles

Many religious traditions have specific expectations regarding marriage and family roles, including the roles of husbands and wives within the marital relationship. In some religious communities, marriage is seen as a sacred institution ordained by a higher power, with specific roles and responsibilities assigned to husbands and wives based on their gender. These expectations may include notions of submission and obedience for wives and leadership and authority for husbands, reflecting traditional patriarchal values.

Restrictions On Leadership Roles

Some religious traditions restrict women from holding leadership positions within religious institutions, such as priesthood or clergy roles. These restrictions are often justified through theological interpretations that prioritize male leadership and authority within religious hierarchies. As a result, women may be excluded from decision-making processes and leadership opportunities within their religious communities.

Challenges To Gender Equality

Religious expectations of gender roles can pose challenges to gender equality and women's empowerment within religious communities. By reinforcing traditional gender norms and hierarchies, these expectations may limit women's agency, autonomy, and opportunities for leadership and self-expression. This can perpetuate gender disparities and contribute to the marginalization of women within religious institutions and societies.

Parenting Roles

Within many religious traditions, there are specific expectations for parenting roles based on gender. Women are often expected to take on the primary caregiving responsibilities for children. In contrast, men are expected to provide for the family financially and serve as authority figures within the household. These roles may be reinforced through religious teachings and cultural practices that prioritize traditional family structures.

Sexuality And Reproductive Health

Religious expectations of gender roles often extend to sexuality and reproductive health. Some religious traditions may promote abstinence until marriage and emphasize procreation within the confines of heterosexual marriage. Discussions about contraception, abortion, and sexual health may be influenced by religious beliefs and teachings, leading to restrictions or prohibitions based on gender.

Spiritual Practices And Rituals

Gender roles can also influence participation in spiritual practices and rituals within religious communities. In some traditions, there may be separate spaces or rituals for men and women, with different expectations for participation and behavior based on gender. Women may be excluded from certain religious rituals or leadership positions. At the same time, men may be expected to lead prayers or perform specific religious duties.

Education And Learning

Religious expectations of gender roles may impact access to education and opportunities for learning within religious communities. In some contexts, women may have limited access to religious education or theological training, leading to disparities in knowledge and leadership opportunities. Men may be prioritized for educational opportunities, particularly within religious institutions that uphold patriarchal values.

Cultural Interpretations

It's important to recognize that religious expectations of gender roles can vary widely based on cultural interpretations and practices within different religious communities. While some traditions may emphasize strict adherence to traditional gender norms, others may adopt more progressive or inclusive interpretations that challenge gender stereotypes and promote greater gender equality.

Intersectionality

Gender expectations within religious communities intersect with other aspects of identity, such as race, ethnicity, class, and sexual orientation. Individuals who belong to marginalized or minority groups may face unique challenges and experiences related to gender roles within religious contexts. Intersectional approaches are essential for understanding the complex interplay between religion, gender, and other dimensions of identity.

Evolution Of Gender Roles

Religious expectations of gender roles are not static. They can evolve over time in response to changing social, cultural, and theological contexts. Some religious communities may reinterpret religious texts and teachings to promote greater gender equality and inclusivity. In contrast, others may cling to traditional interpretations and practices. Understanding the dynamic nature of gender roles within religious traditions is essential for promoting dialogue, reconciliation, and progress toward greater gender equity and social justice.

Navigating religious expectations of gender roles can be complex and challenging, particularly for individuals who may not conform to traditional gender norms or who seek to challenge existing hierarchies and inequalities. It requires critical reflection, dialogue, and advocacy within religious communities to promote greater inclusivity, gender equality, and respect for diverse gender identities and expressions. By challenging restrictive gender roles and advocating for greater gender equity within religious contexts, individuals and communities can work towards creating more inclusive and empowering spaces for all members, regardless of gender.

Personal Stories And Experiences

Growing up is like putting together a puzzle, but not the kind that comes with a neat picture on the box to guide you. Imagine that every piece represents a different part of who you are—your hobbies, your fears, and, yes, your gender identity. When you're young, maybe you don't even realize some pieces are missing, or perhaps you try to force pieces to fit where they don't belong.

YOU ARE THE GENDER YOU ARE - UNDERSTANDING GENDER IDENTITY

Let's talk about Alex, for example. Alex grew up in a small town where everyone seemed to know everyone else's business. As Alex started to understand their own feelings and gender identity, they felt like a puzzle piece that didn't quite fit with the rest of the picture their town had in mind. You see, Alex identified as non-binary, but the town had mostly traditional ideas about gender.

For Alex, it was like trying to complete a puzzle but missing a crucial edge piece. Things like joining team sports or going to school dances felt awkward. Alex was still trying to figure out where they fit into the big picture of life.

Then there's Jamie. Jamie knew from a young age that they were a boy, even though everyone else saw them as a girl. For Jamie, the puzzle seemed upside down. No matter how hard he tried to explain, people just didn't get it. It was like they were looking at a different puzzle altogether.

Life threw some curveballs, and Jamie had to figure out how to rearrange the pieces to make sense. The school wasn't easy. There were bullies, and some teachers didn't understand, but Jamie didn't give up. Eventually, he found friends and even some adults who got it. They helped him turn the puzzle right-side up.

Riley's story is a bit different. Riley is a trans girl who knew where her puzzle piece fit but was afraid to put it there. She had a supportive family but was scared about what other people would say. For Riley, it felt like holding onto a puzzle piece but being too nervous to place it. Finally, one day, she did. She started to live her life as her true self and realized that her piece did fit—just not where others expected it to.

For Alex, Jamie, and Riley, taking responsibility for their actions meant something a little different. Alex had to educate a whole community, Jamie had to stand up for himself, and Riley had to overcome her own fears.

When it comes to figuring out what growing up means, remember it's okay if your puzzle doesn't look like everyone else's. It's yours, after all. Taking responsibility might mean standing up for who you are, educating others, or even accepting yourself. Just like a puzzle, you're a work in progress, and that's perfectly okay.

Puzzles Are Ever-Changing

Let's dig a bit deeper into the lives of Alex, Jamie, and Riley, shall we? Remember, their puzzles are ever-changing, just like anyone else's. And you know what? Puzzles can be rearranged. That's part of growing up and taking responsibility.

Let's circle back to Alex. Being non-binary in a small town felt like trying to solve a puzzle in the dark. People would ask, "Why can't you just be a boy or a girl?" as if it were that simple. To cope, Alex started to read up, joining online communities where people shared their own stories and tips. Realizing that education was key, Alex decided to start a support group at school, a safe place for people to talk openly and honestly. It was like finding a flashlight to help put those puzzle pieces together. Sure, there were hiccups, and not everyone was supportive, but Alex stood firm. They knew this was a part of the puzzle they had to secure.

On to Jamie. Remember how he felt like his puzzle was upside-down? Well, taking responsibility for Jamie meant seeking out information and allies. He talked to counselors, found online forums, and joined a local LGBTQIA+ youth group. Jamie even took it upon himself to educate his teachers on what it means to be transgender. Jamie realized the more he spoke up, the clearer the puzzle became for others, too. Sometimes, pieces fell into place naturally. Sometimes, he had to rearrange a bit. But either way, Jamie's puzzle started to make more sense, both to him and to others.

Now, what about Riley? After taking that big step to live as her true self, she thought her puzzle would be complete. But she learned that there's more to it than just one piece. Riley faced new challenges like dealing with stereotypes and handling questions from curious or insensitive peers. She took responsibility by being patient, educating people, and standing up for herself when needed. Riley even started a blog to share her journey, helping others find where their pieces fit. In doing she discovered that some pieces fit better when you share the experience with others.

You see, each of these stories is about taking control of your own puzzle, no matter what other people think it should look like. Growing up means realizing that you might have to search for some pieces, rotate others, or even flip the whole thing upside-down to understand it better. Taking responsibility isn't just about dealing with your own pieces but also about helping others figure out their puzzles. Sometimes, it's tough, but every piece you place makes the bigger picture a little clearer.

Remember, your puzzle is yours alone, and it's up to you to put it together. It might be confusing or even a little scary, but that's okay. Each piece you add helps you understand more about yourself, and that's what growing up is all about.

Growing Up And Taking Responsibility

Growing up and taking responsibility, focusing on how each person navigates the complex interplay of factors like biology, psychology, and society.

We have Alex again. Remember that support group they started? Well, that group became a safe space for discussing everything from biology to societal expectations. Alex realized that they had to acknowledge not just their own complex feelings but also the broader social norms that people grew up with. In essence, Alex saw that the edges of their puzzle were influenced by society. Still, the core pieces, like hormone levels and emotional well-being, were deeply personal. For Alex, taking responsibility also meant understanding this complex mix and speaking up about it. It was like finding those really weird edge pieces that you don't know where they go until you've figured out more of the puzzle.

Now, let's talk about Jamie. As he navigated his life, he found himself needing to confront not just societal norms but also the medical aspects of being transgender. Hormone therapy was an option Jamie considered carefully. It felt like turning over a hidden puzzle piece and realizing it's a key part of the whole picture. Taking this step wasn't just a personal decision. It also impacted how society viewed him. To take responsibility, Jamie educated himself thoroughly before making any decisions, discussed options with healthcare professionals, and kept his family in the loop.

Finally, we revisit Riley's story. After coming out and beginning to live her life more authentically, Riley also faced medical and psychological questions. Therapy was an essential part of understanding herself, like finding many corner pieces that helped frame the puzzle. Riley felt that society's view, often distorted by stereotypes and misinformation, needed a refresh. She felt responsible for being a part of that change. By sharing her personal journey through blogging, she could influence social perceptions, one reader at a time. For Riley, each blog post was like placing another puzzle piece, not just for herself but for others.

Through all these experiences, it's clear that biology, like hormones and brain structure, plays a part in the puzzle, but it's not the whole picture. Psychology, like one's internal sense of self, is like the colors and patterns that make the puzzle interesting. Society, with its norms and expectations, can be like that friend who's either helping you find the right piece or confusing you by jamming pieces in the wrong spots.

Growing up means recognizing that all these factors contribute to who you are and taking responsibility for navigating them. Sometimes, you might have to educate others or even challenge societal norms. Sometimes, you'll focus on understanding yourself better through therapy or medical options. Your puzzle will always be unique, and it will change over time. That's life. But remember, no matter how complex or intricate your puzzle becomes, every piece is a part of you, and that's worth celebrating.

Time, Patience

The puzzle analogy still holds up because, as we all know, puzzles aren't completed overnight. They take time, patience, and, sometimes, a willingness to walk away and take a breather before tackling it again.

Alex, Jamie, and Riley continue to add more pieces to their puzzles, just like anyone else. And as they grow older, they realize their puzzles will never be truly "complete" because life keeps adding more pieces.

Alex takes their activism to a new level by becoming involved in local politics. They understand that if real change is going to happen, they can't just focus on their individual puzzle. They have to consider the community's puzzle, too. Laws, after all, can act like borders that limit how the pieces fit together for everyone. Alex starts campaigning for inclusive policies and becomes a voice for marginalized communities. It's like they're using their puzzle to help people see the bigger picture, to show that each individual puzzle is a part of a much larger one.

Jamie's life takes a different turn. He decides to go to college far from home, a place where nobody knows his past, and he can introduce himself as he truly is from day one. But Jamie quickly realizes that freedom also comes with the responsibility of being fully independent. There's no one to remind him of healthcare appointments for hormone treatments or to take his wellbeing into consideration. It's all on him now. Being responsible for this new section of his puzzle is daunting but also empowering. He finds a community in college that accepts him for who he is, adding pieces to his puzzle that he never even knew were missing.

Riley, on the other hand, faces a setback. Her blog becomes a target for online trolls who question her identity. It shakes her. Feels like someone just threw all her puzzle pieces up in the air. But instead of stepping back, she takes it as a moment to take responsibility for her platform. She strengthens her resolve and uses the experience to write about the importance of mental health and online safety. It's a difficult period, but one that adds depth to her puzzle, showing her that even setbacks can be important pieces of the overall picture.

Each of these individuals is continually learning that taking responsibility isn't a one-time act. It's an ongoing process. Their puzzles expand and change, just like they do. Alex, Jamie, and Riley learn to adapt to new challenges, finding where new pieces fit and occasionally discovering that some old pieces need to be repositioned.

They realize that while their puzzles are unique, they're interconnected with everyone else's. Taking responsibility means not just finding where your pieces go but also understanding how your puzzle fits into a larger community, society, and even the world.

As they continue to grow and take on new challenges, they keep one key lesson in mind.

The puzzle is never complete, and that's okay. It's the process of adding pieces, reworking sections, and stepping back to appreciate the bigger picture that makes life Rich and meaningful. Whether you're just starting your puzzle or you're well into the process, remember that each piece—no matter how confusing or challenging it may be—adds something invaluable to the masterpiece that is you.

Time Marches On

As time marches on, the lives of Alex, Jamie, and Riley continue to evolve, much like a puzzle growing ever larger and more complex. Sometimes, new pieces appear that they didn't even know existed, and other times, they find that some pieces need to be moved around as they gain a better understanding of their own lives and the world around them.

Alex finds an opportunity to go beyond local politics and gets a chance to talk about gender diversity on a national television panel. It's a big stage, and for the first time, Alex feels the weight of responsibility on their shoulders. They aren't just speaking for themselves anymore. Their voice could impact legislation and public opinion far and wide. It's like going from a small 100-piece puzzle to a sprawling 1,000-piece one. Alex takes time to prepare, consults with mentors, and even does mock interviews. When they finally sit on that panel, they speak clearly and passionately, making sure to place this big, new puzzle piece just right. It's a milestone, an important piece that connects many smaller ones, tying together years of self-discovery and activism.

Jamie, away at college, starts to realize the importance of mental health in his journey. While he loves the freedom and community he's found, he also feels stressed and overwhelmed at times. Jamie understands that it's not just about aligning the outer pieces of his puzzle. The inner ones need attention, too. he started going to therapy and also taking up mindfulness practices. He learns new coping mechanisms that allow him to take better care of himself. For Jamie, these new pieces bring balance and stability to his ever-changing puzzle.

Riley encounters a new challenge as she begins to navigate the world of relationships. Falling in love brings joy but also complexity. She now has to consider another person's feelings, another person's puzzle, and how it fits with her own. When her relationship ends in a breakup, she feels like a big chunk of her puzzle just got ripped away. It's a tough period of self-reflection but also a time for growth. She writes about these deeply personal experiences, adding more layers to her blog. Her followers appreciate this raw honesty, and many reach out to share their own stories. For Riley, this period becomes a new corner section of her puzzle, one filled with emotional highs and lows but essential for the overall picture.

The lessons for Alex, Jamie, and Riley are clear

taking responsibility means addressing not just what's easily visible but also what's under the surface. Sometimes, it involves speaking up for others. At other times, it means taking steps to better understand oneself. It could mean standing in the public eye or facing personal challenges head-on.

Their puzzles continue to be works in progress, influenced by a myriad of factors—biological, psychological, social—and interwoven with those of the people around them. As they place each new piece, they're mindful that they're also contributing to larger conversations, impacting societal perspectives on gender, mental health, relationships, and more.

If you're wondering where your puzzle pieces go or even what they'll look like, know that it's perfectly okay not to have all the answers. The important thing is to keep going, to keep searching for those pieces and finding where they fit, whether in your own life or in the greater tapestry of human experience. The puzzle that is you will always be unique, always evolving, and always worth building.

The Intersection of Biology and Gender

Brain Structure

Growing up is like putting together a big jigsaw puzzle, right? Each piece that snaps into place helps make the full picture. When it comes to figuring out who you are, especially your gender identity, there's many puzzle pieces you can think about.

Let's talk about brain structure first. The brain's kind of like the boss of your body. It helps you think, feel, and even understand who you are. Some experts say that the way your brain is built could play a role in how you see your gender. But remember, it's not like a switch that flips on and off, making you feel a certain way. It's more like one puzzle piece among many.

Your brain is made up of many different parts, each with its own job. You've got the frontal lobe that helps you make decisions and other parts like the amygdala that deal with emotions. Some experts think that these parts might be built a little differently in each person and could have something to do with how you see your own gender.

Imagine your brain is like the corner piece of your puzzle. It's super important and sets the framework for everything else, but it's not the whole picture. Some studies have looked at brain scans to see if there are differences that relate to gender identity. But guess what? It's not a simple "this equals that" kind of thing. Some people with similar brain structures might identify their gender in totally different ways.

Why? Because each brain is like a unique puzzle all on its own. Just because one piece fits in a certain way doesn't mean the whole puzzle will look the same when it's done. While your brain does play a role in who you are, it's not like it comes with a manual that says, "This is your gender."

And here's another thing - You're not just your brain. Your thoughts, feelings, and experiences—those are puzzle pieces, too. And they're shaped by the world around you, not just what's going on in your head.

Neurological Variances

Research has revealed that certain areas of the brain may exhibit structural or functional differences between individuals of different gender identities. For example, studies using neuroimaging techniques such as MRI scans have identified variations in brain anatomy, including differences in the size and connectivity of specific brain regions between cisgender (those whose gender identity aligns with their assigned sex at birth) and transgender individuals.

Brain Activity Patterns

Additionally, studies have shown that patterns of brain activity may differ based on gender identity. Research using techniques such as functional MRI (fMRI) has found differences in brain activation patterns during tasks related to gender perception, body image, and self-referential processing between transgender and cisgender individuals. These findings suggest that the brain may process gender-related information differently based on one's gender identity.

Developmental Influences

The development of gender identity is believed to be influenced by a combination of biological, genetic, hormonal, and environmental factors. During prenatal development, exposure to hormones such as testosterone and estrogen can shape brain development and organization in ways that may influence gender identity later in life. Variations in hormone levels or sensitivity during critical periods of brain development may contribute to differences in gender identity.

Brain Plasticity

The brain exhibits a remarkable degree of plasticity, or the ability to reorganize and adapt in response to experiences and environmental influences. This suggests that factors such as socialization, identity formation, and lived experiences can shape the neural circuits underlying gender identity. As individuals explore and affirm their gender identities, neural networks associated with gender identity may undergo adaptive changes to reflect their true sense of self.

The Brain's "Map" Of Gender Identity

It's as if the brain itself has a map guiding individuals towards their true gender identity. This neural map may integrate various sensory, cognitive, and emotional inputs to construct a coherent sense of self that aligns with one's gender identity. Discrepancies between this internal map and external factors, such as biological sex or societal expectations, can lead to feelings of dysphoria or incongruence.

Implications For Understanding Gender Identity

Understanding the role of brain structure and function in shaping gender identity provides important insights into the diversity and complexity of human experiences. It underscores the biological underpinnings of gender identity and challenges simplistic notions of gender as binary or immutable. Recognizing the neurobiological basis of gender identity contributes to greater acceptance, empathy, and support for transgender and gender-diverse individuals.

Impact Of Hormonal Factors

Hormonal factors during critical periods of brain development can influence the formation of gender identity. For example, exposure to androgen hormones in utero has been linked to the development of male-typical brain structures and behaviors. Variations in hormone levels or sensitivity may contribute to differences in gender identity and expression.

Genetic Influences

Genetic factors also play a role in shaping gender identity. While specific genes associated with gender identity have not been identified, studies have suggested that genetic variations may contribute to differences in brain structure and function that influence gender identity development.

Environmental And Social Influences

Environmental and social factors, such as familial and cultural norms, also shape the development of gender identity. From a young age, individuals are socialized into gender roles based on societal expectations and cultural norms, which can influence the expression of gender identity.

Non-Binary And Genderqueer Identities

The traditional binary understanding of gender (male/female) does not fully capture the diversity of gender identities. Non-binary and genderqueer individuals may identify outside of the binary categories of male and female, and their experiences of gender identity may involve unique neurobiological pathways and processes.

Fluidity And Flexibility

Gender identity can be fluid and may change over time for some individuals. Neurobiological mechanisms underlying gender identity may also exhibit flexibility and adaptability in response to changes in identity or expression.

Intersectionality With Other Identities

Gender identity intersects with other aspects of identity, such as race, ethnicity, sexuality, and disability. The interplay between gender identity and these intersecting identities can influence the neurobiological processes underlying identity formation and expression.

Identity Development Across The Lifespan

Gender identity development is a dynamic process that unfolds across the lifespan. Neurobiological mechanisms underlying gender identity may continue to evolve and change in response to life experiences, personal growth, and self-discovery.

Neurodiversity And Gender Identity

Neurodiverse individuals, such as those with autism spectrum disorder (ASD) or attention deficit hyperactivity disorder (ADHD), may have unique experiences of gender identity that intersect with their neurocognitive profiles. Understanding the intersection of neurodiversity and gender identity can inform more inclusive approaches to supporting individuals with diverse gender identities.

Research Challenges And Future Directions

While research on the neurobiology of gender identity has made significant strides, there are still many unanswered questions and complexities to explore. Future research should adopt interdisciplinary approaches that integrate neuroscientific, psychological, sociocultural, and intersectional perspectives to advance our understanding of gender identity and its neurobiological underpinnings.

Research suggests that brain structure and function play a significant role in shaping gender identity. Neurological variances, developmental influences, and brain plasticity contribute to the intricate interplay between biology, identity, and lived experiences. By exploring the neural mechanisms underlying gender identity, we gain a deeper understanding of the rich diversity of human identity and the importance of affirming and respecting individuals' gender identities.

Relationship Between Biology And Gender Identity

Biology and gender identity are indeed interconnected, much like the pieces of a puzzle forming a complete picture. Let's break it down further.

Core Pieces - Brain Structure And Hormones

Just like the ocean in your beach puzzle, these biological factors are prominent and catch your attention. Brain structure and hormones play crucial roles in shaping aspects of gender identity. For instance, research suggests that certain brain structures may differ between individuals of different gender identities, and hormone levels can influence various aspects of behavior and identity.

Completing The Picture - Other Factors

However, just as a beach scene isn't complete with only the ocean, gender identity isn't solely determined by biology. There are other pieces to the puzzle, like social, cultural, and psychological factors. These pieces, akin to the sky and sand in your puzzle, contribute to the complexity of gender identity. Social factors include upbringing, cultural norms, and societal expectations, while psychological factors encompass individual experiences, beliefs, and self-perception.

Intersectionality - Adding Depth

Additionally, the puzzle of gender identity is further enriched by the concept of intersectionality. This means considering how various aspects of identity, such as race, ethnicity, class, sexuality, and disability, intersect and influence one's experience of gender. Just as different puzzle pieces create depth and complexity in the final image, intersectionality adds layers to our understanding of gender identity.

Unique Arrangements - Individual Differences

Finally, like assembling a puzzle, each person's experience of gender identity is unique. While there may be common patterns or trends, no two puzzles are exactly alike. Similarly, individuals may have different combinations of biological, social, and psychological factors shaping their gender identity, leading to diverse expressions and experiences across the gender spectrum.

While biological factors like brain structure and hormones are significant pieces of the puzzle in understanding gender identity, they do not tell the whole story.

The complete picture also includes social, cultural, psychological, and intersectional factors, all contributing to the complexity and diversity of gender identities.

Understanding The Multifaceted Influences On Gender Identities

In our exploration of gender identities, it's crucial to recognize the intricate tapestry woven by various social, cultural, psychological, and intersectional factors. Let's delve deeper into how each of these influences contributes to the rich diversity of gender experiences.

Social Factors

Social factors encompass the norms, expectations, and interactions within society. From family dynamics to peer influences and media representations, socialization processes shape individuals' understanding and expression of gender. These norms and expectations can influence everything from how we dress to the roles we assume in relationships and careers. Social factors provide the framework within which individuals navigate their gender identity, whether conforming to or challenging societal norms.

Cultural Factors

Cultural factors play a significant role in shaping beliefs, values, and practices related to gender. Different cultures have varying concepts of gender roles, expressions, and identities, each with its own set of traditions and customs. Cultural practices, rituals, and symbols often reflect and reinforce these gender norms, influencing individuals' sense of self and belonging within their cultural context. Understanding cultural diversity is essential for appreciating the complexity of gender identities across different societies.

Psychological Factors

Psychological factors delve into the individual experiences, thoughts, and feelings related to gender. This includes aspects such as self-awareness, self-esteem, and identity development processes. Individuals may grapple with gender dysphoria or internalized stereotypes as they navigate their gender identity journey. Psychological theories offer insights into how individuals learn and internalize gender norms, shedding light on the complexities of gender identity formation and expression.

Intersectional Factors

Intersectionality acknowledges the interconnected nature of social identities and experiences, recognizing that individuals hold multiple intersecting identities that shape their lives. Factors such as race, ethnicity, class, sexuality, and disability intersect with gender to influence individuals' experiences of privilege, oppression, and marginalization. Intersectionality underscores the importance of recognizing and addressing the unique challenges faced by individuals at the intersections of various identities. By centering intersectionality in our understanding of gender, we can strive towards more inclusive and equitable societies.

These multifaceted influences interact and intersect to shape individuals' understanding, expression, and experience of gender identity. By acknowledging and exploring these diverse influences, we can better appreciate the complexity and diversity of gender identities. Moreover, by addressing systemic inequalities and injustices, we can work towards creating more inclusive and affirming environments where every individual can thrive authentically.

Self-Acceptance

Self-acceptance serves as a crucial framework for navigating the intersection of biology and gender identity, akin to having the puzzle box lid with the complete picture. Here's how self-acceptance fits into the biology-gender intersection

Understanding and Embracing Biological Diversity

Self-acceptance allows individuals to acknowledge and embrace the diversity of biological factors that contribute to gender identity. This includes recognizing that there is not a single "correct" or normative biological configuration for gender but rather a spectrum of variations. With self-acceptance, individuals can affirm their own unique biology and understand that it is a valid part of their identity, regardless of how it aligns with societal expectations or norms.

Navigating Gender Dysphoria and Body Acceptance

For transgender and gender non-conforming individuals, self-acceptance plays a pivotal role in navigating experiences of gender dysphoria and achieving body acceptance. Gender dysphoria refers to the distress caused by a misalignment between one's assigned sex at birth and their gender identity. Through self-acceptance, individuals can cultivate compassion and understanding towards their bodies, recognizing that their gender identity is valid and deserving of affirmation, regardless of physical characteristics.

Resisting Societal Pressures and Stereotypes

Self-acceptance empowers individuals to resist societal pressures and stereotypes related to gender and biology. In a world that often imposes rigid gender norms and expectations based on biological sex, self-acceptance allows individuals to challenge these norms and assert their authentic selves. By embracing their gender identity and advocating for their right to self-determination, individuals can carve out space for diverse expressions of gender beyond traditional binaries.

Fostering Resilience and Well-being

Self-acceptance is foundational to fostering resilience and well-being in the face of societal stigma and discrimination. By cultivating self-compassion, individuals can weather challenges and setbacks related to their gender identity with greater ease and resilience. Self-acceptance also facilitates connection with supportive communities and resources, providing vital sources of affirmation and validation.

Promoting Advocacy and Social Change

Finally, self-acceptance fuels advocacy efforts and drives social change by empowering individuals to speak out against injustice and advocate for greater visibility, recognition, and rights for marginalized gender communities. By embracing their own identities with pride and authenticity, individuals inspire others to do the same, contributing to a more inclusive and affirming society for all gender-diverse individuals.

Exploring Identity Fluidity

Self-acceptance allows individuals to explore and embrace the fluidity of gender identity. This includes recognizing that gender identity can evolve and shift over time and that it is okay to embrace changes in one's understanding of self. Self-acceptance facilitates the exploration of diverse gender expressions and identities without judgment or self-doubt.

Seeking Affirming Healthcare

Self-acceptance empowers individuals to seek out affirming healthcare that respects and validates their gender identity. This includes accessing gender-affirming medical interventions such as hormone therapy or gender-affirming surgery, as well as mental health support tailored to the specific needs of gender-diverse individuals. Self-acceptance enables individuals to advocate for their healthcare rights and advocate for culturally competent and affirming care.

Building Supportive Relationships

Self-acceptance fosters the cultivation of supportive relationships with friends, family, and communities that affirm and validate one's gender identity. By embracing their own identity with confidence and authenticity, individuals can attract and maintain relationships that celebrate their true selves. Self-acceptance also allows individuals to set boundaries and prioritize relationships that uplift and affirm their gender identity.

Empowering Self-Expression

Self-acceptance liberates individuals to express their gender identity authentically and without inhibition. This includes experimenting with different forms of self-expression, such as clothing, hairstyles, and mannerisms, that reflect one's inner sense of gender. Self-acceptance encourages individuals to express themselves boldly and unapologetically, challenging societal norms and stereotypes in the process.

Navigating Legal and Institutional Challenges

Self-acceptance equips individuals with the resilience and determination to navigate legal and institutional challenges related to gender identity. This includes advocating for legal recognition of gender identity, challenging discriminatory policies and practices, and seeking recourse in cases of discrimination or harassment. Self-acceptance empowers individuals to assert their rights and demand justice in the face of systemic barriers and inequalities.

Celebrating Intersectional Identities

Self-acceptance celebrates the richness and complexity of intersectional identities, recognizing that gender intersects with other aspects of identity, such as race, ethnicity, sexuality, disability, and more. This includes embracing and affirming the unique experiences and perspectives of individuals with intersecting identities and advocating for greater inclusivity and equity within broader social justice movements.

Cultivating Inner Peace and Fulfillment

Ultimately, self-acceptance fosters inner peace, fulfillment, and a sense of wholeness by aligning one's external expression with one's internal sense of self. By embracing their gender identity with love and compassion, individuals can live authentically and in harmony with their true selves, leading to greater happiness and well-being.

Self-acceptance serves as a guiding light in navigating the intersection of biology and gender identity, empowering individuals to embrace their unique selves, resist societal pressures, foster resilience, and advocate for social change. Through self-acceptance, individuals can affirm the validity of their gender identities and create space for greater diversity and inclusion within society.

Defining Someone's Gender Identity

72

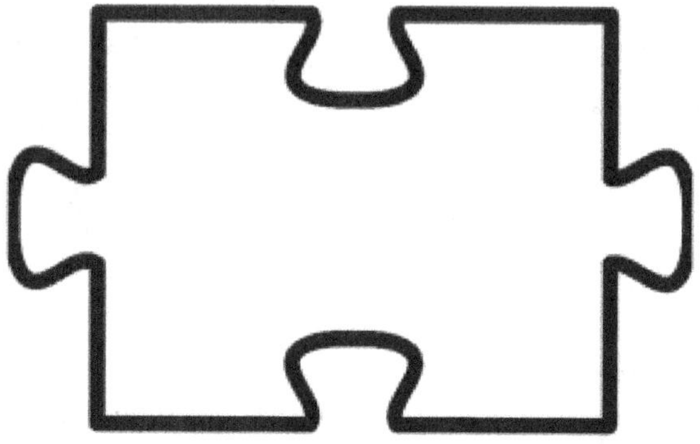

YOU ARE THE GENDER YOU ARE - UNDERSTANDING GENDER IDENTITY

The thing to remember is no one else gets to define someone's gender identity. It's a personal journey, and it's different for everyone. Some people might take a while to figure it out, and that's totally fine. Others might know from a young age. Either way, it's a big part of who someone is, and it's theirs to discover.

Personal Autonomy

At the heart of understanding gender identity is recognizing and respecting individuals' autonomy over their own experiences and self-perception. Just as each person has unique thoughts, feelings, and perspectives, so too do they have the right to define and express their gender identity in a way that feels authentic to them. This autonomy extends to all aspects of gender expression, from pronoun usage to presentation and beyond.

Respecting Diversity

Gender identity is a deeply personal and multifaceted aspect of human experience, and it manifests in a myriad of ways across diverse individuals and communities. By acknowledging that there is no one-size-fits-all definition of gender identity, we honor and celebrate the richness and diversity of human expression. This recognition fosters inclusivity and creates space for individuals of all genders to thrive and be seen and heard.

Embracing Fluidity

Gender identity is not static but rather fluid and dynamic, evolving over time in response to individual growth, self-discovery, and life experiences. Some individuals may have a clear sense of their gender identity from a young age. In contrast, others may undergo a journey of exploration and discovery over time. Embracing this fluidity means accepting that gender identity can be nuanced, complex, and subject to change and that each person's journey is valid and worthy of respect.

Supporting Self-Discovery

Recognizing that gender identity is a personal journey encourages a supportive and affirming environment where individuals feel empowered to explore and discover their authentic selves. This support may involve providing access to resources and information, offering emotional validation and encouragement, and creating spaces that are free from judgment or pressure. By fostering an environment of acceptance and affirmation, we empower individuals to embrace their gender identity with confidence and pride.

Challenging Stereotypes And Expectations

The understanding that no one else gets to define someone's gender identity challenges harmful stereotypes and societal expectations that seek to limit and constrain individuals based on their assigned sex at birth. By rejecting rigid gender norms and embracing the diversity of gender expression, we dismantle oppressive systems and create a more inclusive and equitable society where everyone can live authentically and free from discrimination.

Recognizing that gender identity is a deeply personal journey, unique to each individual, is essential for promoting autonomy, diversity, and inclusivity within our communities. By honoring and respecting each person's self-definition, we create a world where everyone can explore, discover, and embrace their gender identity with dignity and pride.

The Psychology of Gender

Understanding the psychological aspects of gender identity. Think of your mind like a puzzle master. It's constantly working, figuring out which pieces go where and why. Your psychology—the way you think, feel, and understand yourself—is a big part of that.

Self-Concept

This is your mind's way of understanding who you are. It's like the picture on the puzzle box that helps guide you. From a young age, you start forming ideas about yourself. You notice how people talk about girls and boys, what they're "supposed" to like, and how they're "supposed" to act. This can influence how you see yourself, but remember, it's just one piece of the puzzle.

Imagine you've got this big puzzle box, right? On the front, there's a picture. That picture is kind of like your self concept—it shows you what the finished puzzle is supposed to look like. It's your guide, your blueprint. When you're a little kid, that picture might be super simple, maybe just some basic shapes and colors. As you grow, the picture gets more detailed and more complex.

how does that picture start forming? Well, from the moment you're born, people are putting pieces into your puzzle box. Maybe your family says, "Boys don't cry," or "Girls should be sweet and polite." Teachers, friends, TV shows, they all add pieces, too. These pieces shape the picture on your puzzle box, telling you what you "should" be like if you're a boy or a girl—or at least what people expect.

But here's the thing, your self-concept isn't just what other people think. It's also built from your own experiences, feelings, and ideas. Maybe you're a girl who loves to play with trucks, or you're a boy who enjoys painting nails. These are your pieces, and they belong in your puzzle. You start to think, "Hey, maybe the picture on my puzzle box doesn't have to look like everyone else's." And that's a big step in understanding your self-concept.

As you get older, you might realize that some of the pieces don't fit anymore. Maybe you were always told that boys play sports, but you've found out you're more into music or art. That's a moment where your self-concept starts to change. It's like you're swapping out a piece to make the picture more accurate, to make it more "you."

Remember, self-concept is just one piece of the larger puzzle that makes up who you are. It influences how you see yourself, but it doesn't lock you into anything. You've got the power to reshape that picture on the box, to decide what pieces belong and which ones don't.

This is all part of growing up and taking responsibility for your own life. The LARK Code is your trusty guidebook in all of this. Love yourself enough to know that your puzzle is yours alone to build. Accept that some pieces will come from other people, but you choose where they go. Respect yourself by standing firm in who you are, even if your puzzle looks different from someone else's. And always keep getting to Know yourself because the better you understand your own puzzle, the easier it will be to navigate the world around you.

Self-Esteem Is Another Piece

It's how much you value yourself. When your self-esteem is high, it's easier to place other puzzle pieces, like happiness and success, around it. If you're struggling with your gender identity, self-esteem can be a tricky piece to fit in. You might question if you're "doing it right" or if you "fit in" with what people expect.

Let's dive deeper into the self-esteem piece of the puzzle. Imagine self-esteem as one of those corner pieces. You know, the ones that help anchor everything else? When this corner piece is snug and secure, the other pieces—like happiness, friendships, and even how well you do in school—fit more easily around it.

High self-esteem is like having a really clear, well-fitting corner piece. You value yourself, so you're more open to positive experiences and opportunities. You might think, "I'm good at this," or "I deserve to be happy," which makes it easier to find other puzzle pieces that reinforce those good feelings.

But what if you're grappling with your gender identity? Well, that self-esteem corner piece might not fit as snugly as you'd like. Maybe you start doubting yourself. You might think, "Am I getting this right?" or "What if I don't fit into the boy box or the girl box the way others expect me to?" These thoughts can make your corner piece wobbly, and suddenly, the other pieces—like happiness and friendships—aren't as easy to place.

Remember, self-esteem is a puzzle piece that you'll be adjusting and re-adjusting as you grow up and learn more about yourself. And that's completely okay. The aim is to keep making it fit better so your whole puzzle—your whole self—becomes a picture you're proud of.

Identity Formation

Identity formation is like the moment you start seeing the picture take shape. You've got enough pieces in place that you can sort of tell what's going on. For many people, this happens during the teen years, when questions about gender identity might become more urgent. You might ask, "Do I feel like a boy, a girl, both or neither? And what does that mean for me?" You may experiment with different names, pronouns, or clothing styles to see how they fit.

Imagine you've been working on your puzzle for a while now. At it looked like just many scattered pieces, right? But then, as you start to fit more and more together, you notice something awesome—the picture starts to take shape. You can kinda see what it's supposed to be, even if it's not finished yet. That moment? That's a lot like identity formation.

For a lot of folks, this big "aha" moment happens during the teen years. Why? Because that's a time in your life when you're given a bit more freedom to explore and figure out who you are. You're not just accepting the puzzle pieces others hand to you. You're actively looking for your own.

Around this time, you might start having some pretty big questions like, "Do I feel like a boy, a girl, both, or neither? What does that mean for me?" These questions might feel huge and a bit scary, but they're a natural part of putting your puzzle together.

To figure out where these new pieces go, you might start experimenting. Maybe you try out a new name that feels more like "you." Or you switch up your pronouns to see how it feels when people refer to you differently. Perhaps you explore different styles of clothing or haircuts that make you look in the mirror and think, "Yeah, that feels right."

This experimenting isn't just okay—it's super important. It's like picking up a puzzle piece, eyeballing it, and then trying it in different spots to see where it fits best. Sometimes, you'll get it wrong, and that's alright. The important thing is you're actively involved in figuring out your own picture.

And guess what? Your puzzle isn't set in stone. As you grow and change, it's totally normal for the picture to evolve, too. Maybe a piece that fit perfectly when you were 13 doesn't make as much sense at 16. And that's okay! Just like you'd rearrange pieces in a puzzle, your identity can shift and adjust as you learn more about who you are.

don't be afraid to ask those big questions and to try new things. It's all part of forming an identity that makes you say, "Yep, that's me!" when you look at your life's puzzle.

Gender Roles.

Gender roles are the expectations society has for you based on your perceived gender, like an outline that someone else drew on your puzzle. Society says things like, "Boys should be tough" or "Girls should be nurturing." These roles can confuse you, making you question where certain pieces go. Maybe you're a boy who likes to nurture and care for others or a girl who's really good at sports. Where do those pieces fit? Well, they fit where you feel they should. That's your puzzle, after all.

Imagine you've got your puzzle spread out in front of you, and you're doing your best to put it together based on the picture you see on the box. But then, someone comes along with a marker and starts drawing an outline around where they think certain pieces should go. They're trying to help, maybe, but suddenly, your puzzle has this extra layer of guidelines that you didn't ask for. This outline? That's what gender roles are like.

Society has its own set of ideas about what boys should do and what girls should do. "Boys should be tough and never cry." "Girls should be nurturing and like playing with dolls." These roles are like that unwanted outline drawn on your puzzle. They're guidelines that society tries to impose on you, but they can really mess with your groove. They might even make you doubt where you were going to place your pieces.

Let's say you're a boy who likes taking care of others. You're empathetic, compassionate, and nurturing. Society's outline might make you wonder, "Does this piece even belong in my puzzle?" Or maybe you're a girl who's amazing at sports. You're strong and competitive, and you love the thrill of the game. You might think, "Wait, does this piece fit here or there?"

The answer is simpler than you might think. The pieces fit wherever you feel they should. It's your puzzle, and you're the one who has to look at the completed picture for the rest of your life. if you're a nurturing boy, then place that piece proudly. If you're a sporty girl, go ahead and make that part of your picture. It's all about where these pieces fit for you, not where someone else thinks they should go.

Remember, you're growing up, and part of that process is taking responsibility for your own puzzle. Gender roles are just outlines that other people have drawn—they don't have to control where you put your pieces. Using the LARK Code—Love, Accept, Respect, Know—can help guide you in placing each piece exactly where it feels right for you, regardless of what anyone else's outline says.

And don't forget, your puzzle is always evolving. Pieces may shift as you grow, learn more, and have new experiences. And that's completely okay. Remember, there's no one right way to solve a puzzle, especially one as important as your own life.

Exploration Of How Individuals Come To Understand And Express Their Gender.

How people figure out and show their gender identity. Picture this - your puzzle isn't just made up of pieces you find in a box. You also get to draw some of your own pieces. That's a lot like how individuals come to understand and express their gender. It's an active process, like being both a puzzle solver and an artist.

From when you're really young, you start gathering pieces. Maybe your family says, "Look at our strong boy!" or "What a pretty girl!" These are the early pieces you're handed. But as you grow older, especially during your teen years, you begin to question those early pieces. You ask yourself, "Do these really fit in my puzzle?"

Let's zoom in on those early years and the pieces you collect as a young kid. Imagine you're given a puzzle box, but instead of picking it out yourself, it's handed to you by your family. The picture on the front might show a "strong boy" or a "pretty girl," and your family is enthusiastic about it. "This is what the picture should look like," they say. Those early comments and labels? They're the corner and edge pieces you start with. They help you build an initial framework for your puzzle.

As a young kid, you might not question these pieces too much. After all, you trust your family, right? They're the experts on puzzle-building, or so it seems. you start fitting together the puzzle based on that initial outline. You place pieces that align with being that strong boy or pretty girl because those are the pieces you were first handed. It feels simple enough, and you might even feel like you're making good progress on your puzzle.

But then, the teen years hit, and suddenly, those early pieces don't seem as certain anymore. It's like you suddenly notice there are other puzzle boxes with different pictures, and you wonder, "Wait a minute, what if my pieces could fit into a different picture altogether?"

This is the moment when you start to question those first pieces. You look at them and think, "Do these actually fit in my puzzle? Or were they just convenient pieces to start with?" It's like you take a step back and squint at the puzzle you've started to build. Maybe you see gaps or areas where the pieces don't quite align like you thought they did.

For the first time, you realize you have options. You can rearrange some of those early pieces, swap them out for new ones, or even toss some aside and draw your own. This questioning is healthy and totally normal. It's a sign you're growing up and starting to take responsibility for your own life, including your understanding of your gender.

As you move through your teen years, give yourself permission to question those early pieces. It doesn't mean you're rejecting your family or your past. It means you're becoming your own person. You're starting to figure out what your puzzle actually looks like, not just completing the picture someone else started for you.

-his questioning phase is like a treasure hunt. You start to explore new territories. Maybe you read books or articles, watch videos, or talk to people who feel the same way you do. You might even seek out role models who defy gender norms. These explorations give you new pieces to consider, ones you find for yourself.

Treasure Hunt Phase.

you've begun to question those initial puzzle pieces, and you decide it's time to go on an adventure. Think of it like you've found a hidden map in your puzzle box, suggesting there might be more pieces out there you never knew existed. Intrigued, you set out to explore new territories—places you've never been to on your puzzle journey.

How do you explore? Maybe you start by reading books or articles that talk about different experiences of gender. Each page turned, and each article read is like digging a little in the sand and finding new, shiny pieces to consider. These pieces might be different shapes and colors than what you're used to, but that's what makes them so exciting. They offer new possibilities for your puzzle.

Watching videos can be another eye-opening experience. Whether it's TED Talks, documentaries, or YouTube channels dedicated to gender diversity, each video gives you more information and perspective. It's like you're meeting other treasure hunters along the way who show you the unique pieces they've found. These can be inspiring and make you think, "Hey, I want to find pieces like that for my puzzle too!"

Talking to people who feel the same way you do is like joining a treasure-hunting team. You share maps, compare pieces, and even swap stories about the cool areas you've explored. In these conversations, you might realize that many people are going through the same journey as you. You're not alone. You're part of a community of explorers, all looking to complete their own unique puzzles.

Role models who defy gender norms are like legendary treasure hunters. They've been on this journey for a while, and they've got puzzles that look nothing like the standard pictures. They show you that it's not just okay but awesome to have a puzzle that's uniquely yours. Observing them helps you imagine new layouts for your own puzzle, ones you hadn't even considered before.

The pieces you discover during this treasure hunt phase are special because you find them yourself. They're not handed to you. you actively seek them out. This makes them incredibly valuable as they become a part of your evolving puzzle. And because you've taken the responsibility to find these pieces, they hold a lot of meaning and fit in a way that feels right for you. Remember, you're growing up, and part of that growth is taking responsibility for discovering who you are, one treasure hunt at a time.

During this time, you might also play around with how you express your gender. This could mean changing up your wardrobe, adopting new pronouns, or even choosing a new name. It's like you're sketching out new puzzle pieces to see how they might fit into your bigger picture.

And Here's The Cool Part

you're allowed to try these pieces out without committing to them. Maybe you thought a certain piece fit well, but over time, you realize it doesn't look as great as you thought. No big deal! Your understanding of your own gender is a journey, not a one-time decision. You can keep sketching and erasing pieces as you figure things out.

You got it! imagine you've just come back from your treasure hunt, and you're eager to try out these new, shiny pieces you've found. You're excited but also a little unsure. Where do these pieces fit? Do they even belong in your puzzle at all? The awesome news is you don't have to decide right away. You can try them out without any strings attached.

Think of it like having a puzzle piece that's made of erasable material. You place it in one spot, step back, and look at how it fits with the others. Maybe you're like, "Wow, this piece is awesome! It fits perfectly!" But as you keep working on your puzzle, you might notice that the piece doesn't blend as well as you initially thought. Maybe it clashes with other pieces, or maybe you find a piece that fits even better.

That's totally okay! The erasable material means you can make changes. You can take that piece out, erase its edges, and reshape it into something that fits better. Or, you can take it out entirely and go on another treasure hunt to find a piece that feels more 'you.'

This idea of 'trying out' pieces is super important, especially as you're growing up and learning more about yourself. It's like giving yourself permission to make mistakes, to experiment, and to learn. It's acknowledging that figuring out your gender is a journey, one that involves some trial and error. No one gets their puzzle right on the first try, and that's perfectly fine.

Your understanding of your own gender isn't set in stone. it's more like clay that you can mold and remold as you go along. As you get older, you might find that the picture your puzzle makes changes in ways you didn't expect, and that's part of the excitement. You're not locked into any decisions. you're free to explore, adapt, and evolve.

It's Your Puzzle, Your Rules.

You're the one who decides which pieces stay and which ones go, which ones get reshaped, and which ones you'll hunt for next. You're the artist and the puzzle-builder in charge of creating your own unique masterpiece as you grow and take responsibility for your life. So go ahead, try out those new pieces, and see where they lead you. There's no right or wrong way to complete your puzzle, just your way.

This exploration is often a mix of excitement and, let's be real, a bit of confusion or even fear. But that's okay! No puzzle was ever completed without a little trial and error. Plus, you're not alone. Many people, whether they're your age or older, are still figuring out where their pieces go. And they're realizing that it's okay to redraw the lines or even to create an entirely new piece that's a better fit. You're standing there, looking at your puzzle with all these new, shiny pieces you found on your treasure hunts. It's a mixed bag of emotions. On one hand, you're thrilled because these new pieces open up a world of possibilities. They could redefine the entire look of your puzzle! On the other hand, you're also kinda nervous, maybe even a bit scared. After all, what if you place a piece, and it messes up the whole thing?

Here's the thing—emotions like excitement and fear are two sides of the same coin, and they're both super normal when you're exploring your gender identity. Think of them as your puzzle-building buddies. Excitement is like a friend who's always encouraging you to try a new piece, cheering you on. Fear, on the other hand, is the cautious buddy who makes you double-check before placing a piece just to be sure. Both are helpful in their own ways. They keep you balanced.

Trial And Error.

No one ever completed a puzzle by placing each piece perfectly the first time around. You're gonna have moments where you fit a piece, step back, and think, "Yikes, that's not right." But guess what? That's how you learn. That's how you figure out which pieces truly belong and which ones need reshaping or replacing. Mistakes aren't setbacks. they're lessons in disguise.

And hey, don't forget—you're not the only one on this puzzle-building journey. There are people your age, younger, older, you name it, who are also fumbling with pieces, trying to see where they fit. Even adults who seem like they've got it all figured out are often still exploring. You'll find that many are still redrawing their lines, reshaping old pieces, or even carving out entirely new ones. And that's super encouraging because it means you're part of a whole community of explorers.

It's More Than Okay To Be A Work In Progress.

In fact, it's awesome because it means you're alive, growing, and taking responsibility for your own puzzle. So go ahead, feel that mix of excitement and fear, make some mistakes, learn from them, and remember—you're in good company. This puzzle of yours is a lifelong project, and every piece you place, whether it stays or goes, adds to the incredible, unique masterpiece that is you.

as you grow up and take responsibility for building your own unique puzzle, remember it's an ongoing process. And it's perfectly fine if your puzzle doesn't look like anyone else's. After all, it's yours, and the most important thing is that the finished picture makes you happy.

The Role Of Self-Discovery And Self-Acceptance In The LGBTQIA+ Journey

When you're putting together the puzzle that is you, self-discovery and self-acceptance play starring roles. These are like the basic skills every good puzzle-builder needs - being able to spot a corner piece or knowing when to rearrange sections to make everything fit better.

Self-Discovery

Self-discovery is like that phase when you're flipping over all the puzzle pieces to see their colors and shapes clearly for the first time. It's the treasure hunts, the trial and error, and the constant questioning. You're asking, "Is this who I am?" and "How do I feel about that?" You're gathering all these different pieces—from how you understand your gender to how you express it—and trying to see how they might fit together. You're also looking at what makes you different, what makes you similar, and what makes you uniquely you. Self-discovery can be thrilling, but it can also be kinda messy. But hey, what treasure hunt isn't?

Imagine you're looking at a pile of flipped-over puzzle pieces. Each piece represents a different part of you—your likes, dislikes, fears, hopes, and, yes, your gender identity. In this self-discovery phase, you're picking up each piece, one by one, and really examining it. You're asking yourself questions that maybe you've never thought to ask before.

For example, when you pick up a piece that's linked to gender, you might question, "Why do I feel more comfortable in these clothes?" or "Why does it feel so good when someone uses my chosen pronouns?" These questions help you understand the color and shape of each piece. Maybe you discover that a piece you thought was just sky blue has little flecks of gold you never noticed. It's a deep dive into understanding the different elements that make you you.

It's Also About Comparisons.

You're looking at your pieces and then glancing over at other people's puzzles to see how yours is similar or different. Maybe you see someone with pieces that look a lot like yours but are arranged differently. This can make you wonder, "Hey, could my pieces fit like that too?" But here's the catch—just because your pieces may look similar to someone else's doesn't mean they'll fit the same way in your puzzle. And that's totally fine!

But yeah, self-discovery isn't all rainbows and sunshine. Sometimes, you pick up a piece that's confusing or makes you uncomfortable. Maybe it's a piece that society has told you shouldn't be in your puzzle. It might take time to figure out where it fits, or if it fits at all. That's the messy part. You might put it back down, pick it back up, turn it around a dozen times, and still not know where it goes. But remember, it's okay not to have all the answers right away.

Dynamic Process

The thing to keep in mind is that self-discovery is a dynamic process. What do we mean by dynamic? Well, it's always changing. A piece that fits in one corner today might make more sense in the middle tomorrow. As you go through different experiences, meet new people, and learn more about the world and yourself, your pieces might shift and change shape.

And just like any good treasure hunt, self-discovery is packed with moments of 'Aha!' and 'Hmm, maybe not.' It's a thrilling ride because every discovery, whether clear or messy, adds a new layer of understanding to your life's puzzle. So keep flipping those pieces, keep asking questions, and keep being your awesome, evolving self.

Self-Acceptance.

This is the part where you start liking the picture that your puzzle is forming, even if it's not complete yet. It's saying, "Okay, this is me, and that's pretty awesome." Self-acceptance is like gluing down the puzzle pieces you know for sure belong, making them permanent parts of your picture. Sure, there might be spaces and gaps, but that's okay. It just means there's room to grow.

Suppose self-discovery is about flipping over and examining your puzzle pieces. In that case, self-acceptance is when you start feeling good about how those pieces are coming together. You're looking at the layout - maybe it's half-finished or even just a quarter, but you start to think, "Hey, this is starting to look pretty cool."

Self-acceptance doesn't mean you have every piece in place or that you've figured out the entire picture. No way that'd be like expecting to complete a thousand-piece puzzle in an afternoon! What it does mean is that you're okay with the pieces you've put down so far. You might even say, "These pieces? They're not moving. They're a part of me, and that's awesome." It's like gluing those pieces down on the board so they become a permanent part of your life's picture.

The Spaces And Gaps?

Those are important, too. Just because there's an empty space doesn't mean something's wrong. In fact, those spaces are exciting opportunities. Think of them as placeholders for future adventures, lessons, and discoveries. Maybe you'll find a piece next week that fits perfectly into that gap. Or maybe a piece you've been holding onto but didn't know where to place suddenly makes sense. Those gaps remind you that you're still growing, still learning, and still becoming the person you're meant to be.

Self-acceptance is especially important in the LGBTQIA+ journey. Why? Well, sometimes the world tries to tell you that your puzzle should look a certain way or that some pieces don't belong. But self-acceptance helps you stand your ground. It tells you that your puzzle is yours and yours alone to assemble. Whether you identify as lesbian, gay, bisexual, transgender, queer, intersex, asexual, or any other part of the rainbow, self-acceptance says, "I am who I am, and that's something to be proud of."

And remember the LARK Code? Love, Accept, Respect, Know? When you're in the self-acceptance zone, you're really living the "Accept" and "Respect" parts of that code. You're learning to accept yourself, even the pieces you're still unsure about. And you're respecting yourself by allowing your puzzle to be uniquely yours, even if it's not what others expect.

When you look at your puzzle, even if it's still a work in progress, give yourself a pat on the back. Those pieces you've glued down, those gaps you're excited to fill, they're all part of the awesome journey that's making you who you are. And that, right there, is what self-acceptance is all about.

In the LGBTQIA+ journey, self-acceptance can be both empowering and challenging. Why? Because you're dealing with pieces that might not fit neatly into society's puzzle outline. The world has its own idea of what a "normal" puzzle should look like, but here's the thing

there's no one correct way to be human, just like there's no one correct way to finish a puzzle.

In this phase, you're coming face-to-face with some really personal stuff. Maybe you're grappling with your sexual orientation or gender identity, or maybe you're learning how to express your gender in a way that feels true to you.

These are pieces of your puzzle that society often has strong opinions about, but remember, your puzzle isn't for society. It's for you.

When you pick up a piece that represents something society might not easily accept—like being transgender, non-binary, or genderfluid—you're faced with a choice. You can try to hide that piece, or you can say, "You know what? This piece is a part of me, and it belongs in my puzzle."

And What About "Respect"?

Well, respecting yourself means giving yourself the freedom to be authentic. It means saying, "This is who I am, and that's not just okay, it's great." Respecting yourself might also mean setting boundaries and standing up for who you are, even when others might not understand or agree. It's about respecting your own experiences, feelings, and identity and understanding that you deserve to be treated well, both by others and by yourself.

Being honest about who you are takes a lot of guts. Why? Because you're challenging norms, you're challenging expectations, and sometimes, you're even challenging people's beliefs. But here's a secret

Each time you place a piece that's authentically you, you're not only adding to your own puzzle, you're also sending a message to everyone else who's working on theirs. You're telling them, "Hey, it's okay to be different. It's okay to be you."

in the grand scheme of things, self-acceptance is like a big, bold statement that you're making with your puzzle. You're saying, "This is me, take it or leave it, but I'm not changing who I am to fit your idea of what my puzzle should look like." And that, right there, is pretty awesome.

Both Self-Discovery And Self-Acceptance Are Ongoing Processes.

You don't just find out who you are and instantly accept it all in one day. Nah, it's more like a journey with lots of rest stops, detours, and scenic views along the way. And as you're growing up, these aspects become especially important because you're starting to take more responsibility for your own life and choices. Your puzzle won't complete itself, after all.

Self-discovery and self-acceptance are definitely not one-and-done deals. Think about your puzzle. As you grow and experience new things, you find more pieces. Some might fit snugly into your existing picture, while others might make you think, "Hmm, where does this one go?" Life doesn't stop, and neither does the process of figuring yourself out.

When you're younger, most of your puzzle pieces are handed to you—by family, teachers, friends, and society. They say, "Here, this is what boys or girls are like," or "This is what people your age do." But as you grow older, especially in your teen years and beyond, the responsibility shifts. Now, it's more on you to find your own pieces. It's like the training wheels come off, and you have to figure out how to balance on your own.

Responsibility For Your Life

Taking more responsibility for your life means making choices. Every choice, even the little ones, adds a new detail to your puzzle. Do you stay in the closet or come out? Do you conform to what's expected, or do you break the mold? Do you hold onto pieces that don't really fit anymore just because they're familiar? Making these choices can be scary because it feels like you're drawing permanent lines in your puzzle. But guess what? Most lines can be redrawn. Mistakes can be lessons. Detours can lead to scenic views you'd never expect.

Rest Stops And Scenic Views.

Maybe a rest stop is taking time to reflect or talk to trusted friends or mentors. Maybe it's doing some journaling or soul-searching to figure out how you really feel about something. And scenic views? Those are the moments when everything just clicks, and you feel super sure and happy about who you are. Those views make all the bumps and detours worth it.

When you're taking more responsibility for your life, you're not just finding new puzzle pieces. You're also deciding how and where to place them. And as you fit more pieces together, you'll find that your self-discovery and self-acceptance keep deepening. Your understanding of yourself becomes more nuanced and more detailed—just like how a puzzle looks more complete and beautiful with each added piece.

Yes, it's an ongoing journey, full of ups, downs, and roundabouts. But every twist and turn adds a little more definition to your puzzle, making it more uniquely, authentically you. And that's pretty darn cool if you ask me.

keep flipping those pieces, keep treasure hunting, and keep rearranging your puzzle until it feels right for you. Self-discovery gives you the pieces, and self-acceptance helps you place them with confidence. Both are crucial steps in creating the masterpiece that is uniquely, wonderfully you.

The Role Of Self-Knowledge In The Psychology Of Gender

Self-knowledge plays a big part in understanding your own gender identity, and it's like having a magnifying glass to closely examine each puzzle piece. It helps you see the intricate details, the colors, and how each piece might fit into the bigger picture. But getting that self-knowledge? Ah, that's a journey of its own.

Imagine holding that magnifying glass over each puzzle piece. This isn't just a quick glance. you're really studying each piece's shape, texture, and how its colors blend. Similarly, gaining self-knowledge is a thorough, often slow process. It's not about quick judgments but a series of observations and reflections.

When it comes to gender identity, that magnifying glass of self-knowledge helps you focus on various aspects of yourself. For instance, you might examine how you feel in different social situations. Do you feel more comfortable or authentic when people refer to you with certain pronouns? This observation becomes a key piece of your puzzle, offering a detail you might not have noticed otherwise.

And Let's Talk About Emotions.

They're like the colors on each puzzle piece. Sometimes, these colors are bright and easy to name. Other times, they're more subtle, complex blends. Paying attention to your emotional reactions when exploring your gender identity can offer more clues about who you are. Does wearing a dress make you feel joyful? Does being called "sir" make you uncomfortable? These emotional hues are crucial details for completing your puzzle.

Self-knowledge also involves recognizing your thought patterns. Are there recurring thoughts you have about your gender? Maybe you keep coming back to a specific memory from childhood, or perhaps you frequently daydream about living as a different gender. These thoughts are like the unique shapes of your puzzle pieces, giving you a hint about where they might fit in the larger picture of your identity.

And don't forget, self-knowledge is a treasure that often comes from exploration. You might need to read, chat with others, or even consult experts like therapists to gain insights. Each new piece of knowledge, whether discovered on your own or learned from others, is like adding another piece to your puzzle, helping you see the larger picture more clearly.

However, just like a puzzle isn't completed in a single sitting, self-knowledge is an ongoing process. As you grow and change, you'll likely need to pick up that magnifying glass again and again, reassessing old pieces and examining new ones. This constant revisiting is not just normal. it's a crucial part of the journey, especially as you take on more responsibilities and navigate the complexities of adult life.

Psychological Standpoint

From a psychological standpoint, self-knowledge is understanding your own thoughts, feelings, and actions. In terms of gender, it's asking questions like, "How do I feel when someone calls me by this pronoun?" or "What emotions come up when I wear these types of clothes?" or even, "How do I feel about the gender roles society expects of me?" By asking yourself these questions, you're picking up each puzzle piece for a closer look.

Emotions

When you ponder, "How do I feel when someone calls me by this pronoun?" you're examining the shape of a very specific puzzle piece. Maybe it's one with smooth edges, easily fitting into the broader picture you have of yourself. Or perhaps it's a piece with jagged edges, making you realize it doesn't quite belong where you originally thought. Either way, by asking the question, you gain valuable insight into how that piece contributes to your overall sense of gender identity.

"What emotions come up when I wear these types of clothes?" is another significant question. Here, you're not just looking at the shape of the puzzle piece but also its color and pattern. Does wearing a skirt give you a sense of freedom, adding a splash of bright color to your puzzle? Or does it make you feel restricted, like a piece that's monochromatic and doesn't add much to the overall picture? Your emotional response can help you figure out where this piece might fit or if it fits at all.

"How do I feel about the gender roles society expects of me?" That's like taking a step back and looking at not just one piece but a whole section of your puzzle. Society's expectations are like the corner pieces. They frame a lot but don't define everything within. Maybe you find that these roles feel limiting like they're forcing pieces into spots where they don't truly belong. Or maybe some societal roles actually resonate with you and feel like they fit just right.

By asking yourself these questions, you're doing more than just casual introspection. You're engaging in a form of self-analysis, like a detective closely studying each clue. It's a way to take those puzzle pieces—each representing different aspects of your thoughts, feelings, and experiences—and figure out a layout that feels true to who you are. This is where self-knowledge comes into play, helping you see how everything connects in your unique, complex, and ever-changing puzzle of gender identity.

Self-Examination

As you delve into this self-examination, you're also likely bumping into that complex mix of biological, psychological, and social factors. Maybe you realize that the way you feel doesn't line up with the body you were born with, and that makes you question where that piece fits. Or perhaps you discover that you're really comfortable in roles that society usually reserves for another gender. These are important clues and bits of self-knowledge that help you piece together your unique puzzle. Some pieces might be pretty close to the surface and easy to identify and place. Others might be buried a bit deeper, hidden under layers of biological factors, psychological feelings, and societal expectations.

Biology

Let's talk biology first. If you realize that how you feel doesn't quite match up with the body you were born into, that's like digging up a puzzle piece you hadn't paid much attention to before. Now that it's in your hands, you can't ignore it. It might be a piece that you need to spend more time understanding—how it fits or even if it fits into the bigger picture. Does it go in the corner, in the middle, or does it tell you that maybe you need to rearrange some other pieces, too?

Psychology.

If you find out that you're way comfy in roles that society usually pegs for another gender, that's a game-changer. It's like finding a puzzle piece hidden under the couch that suddenly makes sense in the central part of your puzzle. You're understanding your own mind better, recognizing how you feel and think when you break away from what's "expected." And these psychological insights? They're like glue that can help stick your puzzle pieces in place, making them key parts of who you are.

Society, The Big Influencer.

Society loves to hand out puzzle pieces, telling you, "This goes here, and that goes there." But as you grow and learn, you might decide that the pieces society handed you don't fit at all. Or maybe just a few of them do, and the rest are better off swapped out for pieces that feel more you.

as you're piecing together your puzzle, remember that each layer—biological, psychological, and social—adds complexity but also richness. Each clue you gather, each piece you scrutinize, gets you closer to seeing the full picture. And the more you dig, the more self-knowledge you gain, helping you better understand where each unique piece fits in your one-of-a-kind puzzle.

Ender Theory

Reading up on gender theory is like being handed a guidebook for your puzzle. Maybe it doesn't have the exact picture you're creating, but it's got some solid tips on how to approach the task. It helps you understand the corners, edges, and maybe even some of the more confusing middle sections. You get words and ideas that help you make sense of pieces you've been turning over and over in your hands, not sure where they go.

Talking to people with different experiences is like trading puzzle pieces. They give you a piece of their puzzle, and you give them a piece of yours. Now, that piece might not fit perfectly into your own puzzle, but it can give you new ideas. Like, "Whoa, I never thought a piece like that could even exist!" Or, "Hmm, that piece kinda looks like one of mine but in a different color. I wonder what that means for me?"

And hey, don't underestimate the value of listening to older folks in the LGBTQIA+ community. That's like getting advice from someone who's already completed a similar puzzle. They've been through the whole process—flipping over pieces, trial and error, getting stuck, and eventually figuring it out. Their stories might offer you shortcuts or help you avoid dead-ends. Plus, they can reassure you that it's totally okay for your puzzle to be a work in progress.

The "Know" Part Of LARK?

It's kinda like the toolbox for your puzzle. It gives you different ways to approach your own journey of self-knowledge, different strategies to try, and even some pep talks when you're feeling stuck. All these new perspectives add pieces that enrich your own unique puzzle, helping you see it in a fuller, more complex, but totally awesome way.

But here's the tricky thing, as you grow and change, some of your puzzle pieces might change, too. And that's perfectly fine! Self-knowledge is an ongoing process. The more you learn about yourself, the more you realize there's even more to learn. So you keep asking questions, keep looking for new pieces, and keep trying to fit them into your evolving picture.

Your puzzle isn't some static image that never changes. It's more like a living, evolving piece of art. Imagine it like this - you've got your puzzle mostly together, but then life tosses you a brand-new piece or changes the shape of an old one. Maybe you start a new school, make a new friend, or learn something new about yourself. Suddenly, you're holding this piece and thinking, "Hmm, where does this fit now?"

Because you're growing up and taking on more responsibilities, you're also getting more opportunities to find new pieces. You're joining clubs, taking classes, and meeting people from different backgrounds. All of these experiences are like treasure chests of new puzzle pieces. Some might fit into your puzzle right away, and others might have you scratching your head for a bit.

Don't stress if a piece that used to fit perfectly suddenly feels out of place. That's a totally normal part of growing and learning. Self-knowledge isn't like reaching the end of a race. It's more like walking on a long, winding road with plenty of interesting stops. You keep gathering new pieces, and sometimes, that means you have to rearrange some of the old ones.

It's like the more you know, the more you realize there's to know, you know? That can feel a bit overwhelming at times, but it's also really exciting. Each new piece you find, whether it's a perfect fit or needs some tweaking, adds more depth and color to your puzzle. And the more complex your puzzle becomes, the more interesting and uniquely yours it is.

embracing the constant change in your puzzle isn't just okay. It's a crucial part of the journey. Keep asking those questions and seeking out new experiences. They're all opportunities to add new pieces, rearrange old ones, and get an even clearer picture of the awesome, ever-changing puzzle that is you.

And why is this especially important when you're growing up and taking on more responsibilities? Well, the more you know yourself, the better equipped you are to make choices that are right for you. Whether it's deciding on a career, choosing who to hang out with, or even just picking out your daily outfit, self-knowledge helps you align these choices with who you truly are. And when your choices reflect your true self, the puzzle not only takes shape more easily but also looks more like the picture you want to create.

When you're growing up, it feels like the stakes get higher, doesn't it? You're not just deciding what game to play during recess. You're making choices that start to shape your future. And let's be real, that can be both exciting and kinda scary. But the more you know yourself, the more you can navigate these choices with confidence.

Think about it - if you know what kinds of puzzle pieces make you happy, you're less likely to jam in ones that don't really fit just because someone else thinks they should. Maybe you've always been told you'd be a great lawyer, but you discover you have a passion for art. Knowing that about yourself empowers you to pursue a path that will make you happier in the long run, even if it's not what others expect.

And it's not just about the big stuff like careers. Knowing yourself also helps with the smaller, day-to-day choices. Suppose you understand your own gender identity and are comfortable with it, for instance. In that case, you can express yourself in a way that feels genuine, whether it's through the clothes you wear, the pronouns you use, or the way you interact with others. These may seem like small pieces, but they're super important in making the overall puzzle look and feel like 'you.'

Plus, let's not forget about relationships. As you take on more responsibilities, you also have to manage more complex social situations. Knowing who you are helps you choose friends and partners who respect your puzzle and whose pieces complement yours. You learn to stand your ground and say, "This is me. Take it or leave it," which is a powerful thing.

As you're taking on more adult-like roles and responsibilities, self-knowledge is like your trusty puzzle guidebook. It helps you know where the pieces should go and which pieces to even pick up in the first place. And as you get better at this, you'll find that your puzzle doesn't just come together faster. It also looks more like the awesome, one-of-a-kind masterpiece you're meant to create.

Gender Across Cultures and Time

Examination Of How Gender Roles And Norms Vary Across Different Cultures.

Do you know how some puzzles have different themes, like nature or superheroes? Well, each culture has its own "theme" or way of looking at gender roles and norms. Let's dig into a few examples to see how different these puzzles can be.

Japan

let's look at Japan. You might have heard of the term "salaryman," which is like the ideal adult male role in Japan's work culture. These guys are supposed to be super dedicated to their jobs. On the flip side, women in Japan are often expected to be homemakers, even if they work. It's like their puzzle pieces have been shaped to fit into very specific spots. But hey, things are changing. More and more women are continuing their careers, and some guys are becoming stay-at-home dads. even if a puzzle is mostly set, you can still find new ways to fit the pieces together.

Imagine that in Japan's puzzle, there's a specific spot shaped like a briefcase. That's the "salaryman" role. Guys who fit into this piece are really dedicated to their work, often putting in long hours and even sacrificing family time. It's like they're custom-made to snugly fit into that briefcase-shaped spot in society.

Now, there's another spot in Japan's puzzle that's shaped like a house. Traditionally, this is where women are expected to fit. These women take care of the home, raise the kids, and support their salaryman husbands. even if they have jobs outside the home, there's a strong social push for them to also excel in their roles as homemakers.

But guess what? Puzzles aren't made of stone. they're more like clay. They can change shape over time. In recent years, Japan has been experiencing shifts in these traditional roles. More women are climbing the corporate ladder, starting their own businesses, and even becoming leaders in their fields. Their puzzle pieces are stretching and reshaping to fit into spots that used to be reserved for salarymen.

And it's not just women. Some men in Japan are stepping out of the strict salaryman mold to become more involved at home. They're taking on roles that were traditionally seen as "women's work," like taking care of kids and managing the household. It's like their briefcase-shaped puzzle pieces are becoming more flexible, able to fit into different spots like the house-shaped one.

Being LGBTQIA+ in this changing landscape means there's more room to figure out where your own puzzle piece fits. Maybe it's shaped a bit like a briefcase and a little like a house, or maybe it's a completely different shape altogether. That's totally okay. What matters is that you understand how your piece can fit into the larger puzzle of society while staying true to yourself.

Scandinavia

Now, let's jet-set to Scandinavia—think of countries like Sweden and Norway. Land of Vikings, fjords, and a very different approach to gender roles. Over there, they're really into gender equality. Both men and women are encouraged to work and take care of the home. They even have long paternity leave for dads. It's like their puzzle pieces are made to be interchangeable, fitting in multiple spots without any fuss.

In countries like Sweden and Norway, men and women are encouraged to share responsibilities, both at work and at home. The government even steps in to make this easier. For instance, they have really generous parental leave policies. New moms get time off, sure, but new dads also get paternity leave, encouraging them to be hands-on from the get-go. if we go back to our puzzle analogy, it's like both the 'mom' and 'dad' pieces can fit into the 'caring parent' spot without any issue.

This interchangeable approach isn't just about parenting. It also applies to careers. In Scandinavia, you'll find more women in high-ranking jobs and political positions compared to many other places. Meanwhile, jobs that are traditionally considered "feminine," like nursing or teaching, also attract men. The career piece of the puzzle isn't strictly cut into "male" and "female" shapes. It's more flexible and allows for a mix-and-match.

Being LGBTQIA+ in Scandinavia means you're in a society where the puzzle pieces are already pretty flexible. if you're figuring out your own identity and roles, you've got some room to breathe. It's less about forcing your piece to fit into a pre-cut spot and more about finding multiple spots where you could fit comfortably.

When you think about growing up and taking responsibility for your actions in a place like Scandinavia, it's less about conforming to specific roles and more about embracing a balanced life. The key takeaway? Even if you're a unique shape in this cultural puzzle, there are likely multiple places for you to fit in.

Knowing that you can fit into different parts of life's puzzle makes the journey of self-discovery a lot less stressful.

India

Let's hop on over to India, a country with a really diverse and complex puzzle when it comes to gender roles. Imagine that India's cultural puzzle has traditional spots for men and women, just like many other puzzles around the world. The male pieces are usually shaped to fit into roles like "breadwinner" or "leader." In contrast, the female pieces are more tailored for roles like "homemaker" and "caregiver."

But hold on, India's puzzle has got some extra twists! In certain regions, like the states of Meghalaya and Nagaland, the roles are flipped or shared more equally. Women there often run local markets and are key players in the economy. Their puzzle pieces aren't confined to the home-shaped spot. They also fit perfectly into the business and leadership spots.

And get this

India's puzzle has extra pieces that many other puzzles don't. We're talking about the Hijra community. Hijras are recognized as a third gender in India and have a unique role in society, especially in ceremonies like weddings and births. The puzzle has an additional set of pieces shaped differently than the "male" and "female" ones. Still, they are just as important to completing the overall picture.

Suppose you're LGBTQIA+ and trying to figure out how to grow up responsibly in a society as diverse as India. In that case, you've got to be aware that the puzzle you're part of is super complex. It's not just about finding one spot where your piece fits. It's about understanding that you could fit into multiple spots depending on where you are and who you're with.

Knowing the shape of your own puzzle piece and how it fits into the bigger picture helps you make choices that are right for you. It means respecting traditions and cultural norms but also tecognizing that it's okay for your piece to fit into spots that might not be traditional. Your piece is unique, and that makes the puzzle more interesting and complete.

United States

The whole idea of cultures within cultures is like having a smaller puzzle inside a larger one. Kinda like those Russian nesting dolls, but with puzzles!

Take the United States. On the surface, you might think the U.S. puzzle is pretty progressive. There's a growing acceptance of different gender roles, LGBTQIA+ rights are advancing, and both men and women are found in a variety of careers and lifestyles. You'd think the puzzle pieces are pretty flexible, fitting into many different spots without much hassle.

But then you zoom in, and you realize there are smaller puzzles inside the big one. These could be religious communities, ethnic groups, or even regional cultures. And each of these smaller puzzles might have its own unique set of rules about where each piece should go.

For example, in some religious communities in the U.S., traditional gender roles are still pretty strong. Men are often seen as the head of the household, while women might be encouraged to focus on raising kids and taking care of the home. In these sub-puzzles, the shapes of the pieces haven't changed much over time and still fit into their traditional spots.

Suppose you're LGBTQIA+ and trying to grow up responsibly in this multi layered situation. In that case, you've got a cool but challenging task ahead. You're not just figuring out where your piece fits in one puzzle. You've got to navigate several puzzles at the same time.

How do you do it? It's like being a puzzle piece with the ability to adapt its shape. Sometimes, you'll fit easily into the bigger, more flexible puzzle, and other times, you might need to adjust a bit to fit into a smaller, more traditional one. But remember, no matter where you fit, your piece is a vital part of making each puzzle complete.

What's the takeaway if you're LGBTQIA+ and trying to figure out how to grow up and take responsibility for your actions? Well, understanding that each culture's puzzle is different can help you see that there's not just one "right" way to be a guy, a girl, or anything in between or beyond. You're your own puzzle, and the pieces that make you "you" can fit together in a way that feels right.

Historical Perspectives On Gender Identity And How They Have Evolved.

Way back in ancient times, the puzzle was pretty basic in many cultures.

Picture a really old, hand-carved puzzle where most of the pieces are either square or circle—representing the traditional roles of male and female. In a lot of ancient cultures, like in Greece or Mesopotamia, those squares and circles had their designated spots. The squares, or men, usually fit into roles like "warrior," "hunter," or "leader." The circles, or women, were usually designed to fit into the "homemaker" or "gatherer" slots.

But here's where it gets interesting. Even back then, some cultures recognized that life's puzzle could be more intricate. Take Native American societies as an example. They had this concept of "Two-Spirit" individuals. Imagine these as pieces that are a blend of square and circle, or maybe an entirely different shape altogether, like a star or a triangle.

Two-Spirit people had special roles in their communities that were neither strictly male nor strictly female. They could perform tasks reserved for both men and women and sometimes held unique roles like being spiritual leaders or mediators. In the grand puzzle of their society, these Two-Spirit pieces fit into multiple slots, making the overall picture more complex and more complete.

If you're an LGBTQIA+ individual trying to navigate the modern world's ever-changing puzzle, knowing about these ancient exceptions can be pretty empowering. It's a reminder that puzzles have had diverse pieces for centuries, even if those pieces were sometimes forgotten or pushed to the side in other cultures.

Know that even if your piece doesn't look like the 'traditional' ones, it has a place in the puzzle, just like the Two-Spirit people had in their communities. Your unique shape adds to the richness of the puzzle, making it a more accurate reflection of what society really looks like.

Middle Ages And The Renaissance

Picture this - the puzzle of society has gotten a bit more complex. There are more spots to fill, but the shapes of most of the pieces are still those familiar squares and circles. Men, the square pieces, are still often filling roles like knights, farmers, or tradespeople—basically, the providers. Women, the circle pieces, still mainly fit into the "homemaker," "wife," or "mother" slots.

But guess what? This era had its rule-breakers, too, pieces that didn't quite fit where you'd expect them to. Enter Joan of Arc, a perfect example. She was like a circle piece that said, "Hey, I can fit into that square-shaped warrior spot, watch me!" And she did, leading armies and making a name for herself in a role that was pretty much a square-only zone back then.

Joan of Arc wasn't just challenging the norms for kicks. Her actions had a ripple effect, shaking up society's ideas about where a 'female' puzzle piece could fit. People had to start questioning their assumptions, and even if change didn't happen overnight, the puzzle got a little less rigid because of it.

Suppose you're LGBTQIA+ and sorting through the puzzle of growing up. In that case, folks like Joan of Arc are excellent reminders that it's okay to defy expectations. Your piece might not look like everyone expects it to, but that doesn't mean it can't fit into spots usually reserved for other shapes. And sometimes, by pushing into those spaces, you make it easier for the pieces that come after you to find their own fitting spots.

Now Zoom Up To The 20th Century.

With the rise of LGBTQIA+ movements, feminism, and more understanding of gender as a spectrum, the puzzle pieces are becoming more diverse than ever. Some people don't even fit into traditional 'male' or 'female' spots, and that's okay! The puzzle has expanded to include all kinds of new shapes and sizes.

If you're LGBTQIA+ and trying to figure out what growing up means for you, just remember that the puzzle of gender identity is always changing. The piece that represents you might not have even existed a few decades ago! And that's cool. It's all about figuring out the shape of your own piece and where it fits in today's puzzle.

Growing up can be like figuring out a puzzle, right? And if you're LGBTQIA+ in today's world, the piece that represents you may look really different than the traditional square or circle. Your piece might be a star, a triangle, or even a shape no one's named yet!

Think about it, a few decades ago, many of these unique pieces weren't even recognized as part of the puzzle. People used to think the puzzle was super straightforward, like, "Here are your squares and circles, end of story." But now we know better. The puzzle has a lot more variety, and that's what makes it so cool and interesting.

Figuring out the shape of your own piece might take time, and that's okay. You might need to try fitting into different spots before you find the one that feels just right. And as you're doing that, you're also learning about yourself. You're discovering your interests, your strengths, and even your weaknesses, which are all parts of your unique shape.

And hey, puzzles can be rearranged, right? As you grow, learn, and change, you might find that your piece fits into more than one spot or that it fits differently than it did before. Life's changes—like new friendships, moving to a different place, or learning more about your own identity—can all be opportunities to see how your piece fits into new parts of the puzzle.

If you're LGBTQIA+ and trying to figure out life and responsibility, just remember, you're not alone. The puzzle is big enough for all kinds of pieces, and it's always changing. Stick to the LARK Code

Love yourself, Accept yourself, Respect yourself, and Know yourself. By doing that, you're not only finding your place in the puzzle but also helping to shape it into a more inclusive and beautiful picture.

The Impact Of Culture And Society On An Individual's Perception Of Their Gender

Let's talk about how culture and society can shape the way you see your own puzzle piece, especially when it comes to gender. Imagine you're born into a society where the puzzle only has squares and circles, and you're handed one of those pieces as soon as you arrive. From that moment on, people tell you, "Hey, you're a square, so you fit here," or "You're a circle, so you go there." It's like they're trying to guide your piece into a pre-made slot in the puzzle.

You got it! Let's dig deeper into this puzzle metaphor. So picture yourself born into this society, right? You barely have time to breathe, and bam! You're handed a square or circle piece. This is your starting point, kind of like being given a set of instructions. The adults, the media, your friends—they all start pointing to the spots where your piece "should" go based on whether you're a square or a circle.

Now, why do they do this? Well, it's not just random. These puzzle slots have been formed over generations. They're based on old beliefs and traditions that people just carried forward. So it feels like there's a whole assembly line of folks, maybe well-meaning but sometimes clueless, trying to push you to where they think you belong. It's like a game, but not always a fun one.

These slots aren't just for show, either. They come with sets of behaviors, actions, and even feelings that you're "supposed" to have. Let's say you're handed a square. You might hear things like "Squares are strong," "Squares don't show emotion," or "Squares do this kind of work." The society's message is clear

"Here are the lines and borders where your piece fits. Stick to them."

But here's where it gets really interesting. What if you start to feel like your puzzle piece has some extra corners or curves? What if you feel more like a star, a hexagon, or even a shape that no one's thought of yet? Now, you're faced with a choice. Do you listen to the world telling you to sand down your corners and curves to fit in? Or do you make the bold move to say, "Hey, my piece is different, and that's okay!"

This is a huge deal, especially for someone in the LGBTQIA+ community who might be figuring out that their piece doesn't align with what society handed them. It's like realizing that your piece is part of a whole different puzzle that's way more diverse and colorful than you were led to believe. When you finally understand your unique shape, you can start looking for the places where you really fit, not just the places where people told you to fit.

If you're LGBTQIA+ and navigating the twists and turns of growing up, realizing how culture and society have shaped your perception is like getting a map of the puzzle. This insight helps you recognize why you've felt pushed into certain slots and why it's okay to seek out new ones that genuinely fit you.

These guidelines can come from all over—your family, your school, movies, social media, you name it. For instance, maybe you're told that squares play with trucks and circles play with dolls. Squares should be tough and not cry, while circles should be nurturing and kind. Even if it's not said out loud, these ideas can be all around you, kinda like invisible hands trying to push your puzzle piece into certain spots. Let's break down where these guidelines—or let's call them 'rules'—really come from and how they're like invisible hands pushing your puzzle piece around.

Family

family. Your family is usually the first set of hands that try to place your piece. They've got traditions and beliefs that have been passed down, right? Maybe Grandpa was a square who loved fishing, and Grandma was a circle who baked. So naturally, they might expect you to fit into similar spots. It's like they're handing you a puzzle piece that's been passed down through the family and saying, "Here, this is where you go."

School

You know how it is—schools have their own sets of rules and ideas. Teachers, classmates, and even textbooks can have a say in where your puzzle piece "should" fit. Like, squares might be nudged toward math and science, while circles get pushed toward art and literature. It's another layer of those invisible hands trying to guide you based on old ideas about squares and circles.

Movies And Media?

Oh man, they're big players. Think about the last movie you watched. Were the squares superheroes saving the day? Were the circles princesses waiting for rescue? Even without saying a word, movies can shape our ideas of what it means to be a square or a circle. They create these slots in the puzzle that look super glamorous and perfect, and suddenly, you think, "I need to fit in there."

Social Media

And don't get me started on social media. Instagram, TikTok, you name it—they're all showing off 'ideal' squares and circles. Photoshopped puzzle pieces, if you will. And sometimes, that can make you feel like you've got to change your shape to get likes or approval. It's as if these platforms are invisible hands with megaphones, shouting about where your piece should go and how it should look.

The thing is, all these 'rules' and invisible hands can make you feel pressured, especially if you're LGBTQIA+ and your piece doesn't look like a simple square or circle. You might feel like you're in a tug-of-war, being pulled in directions that don't feel right. But once you realize that these rules aren't the be-all and end-all, you start to see that it's okay for your piece to be different. It's more than okay—it's awesome.

Triangle, Or A Star, Or Some Other Shape

But what if your piece feels more like a triangle, a star, or some other shape altogether? The invisible hands might make you think, "Whoa, maybe there's something wrong with my piece," or "I need to trim my edges to fit better." But here's the real deal - there's nothing wrong with your shape. It's the puzzle that needs to make room, not you, that needs to change.

If you feel like your piece is a triangle, star, or some shape that's not even in the book of geometry yet, it's easy to feel like you're the one who has to change. Those invisible hands—coming from family, school, movies, or social media—might make you think your shape is a "mistake" or a "problem." They might nudge you toward those scissors to start snipping away at your edges.

But hold up. Why should you have to change your shape? Isn't the whole point of a puzzle to have different pieces that come together to make a complete picture? If every piece were a square or circle, that would be a pretty boring puzzle. The unique shapes, like triangles and stars, and whatever you want, add the spice. They're what make the puzzle interesting and awesome.

This feeling that you need to "fit" can be especially tough if you're part of the LGBTQIA+ community. You might see all these traditional squares and circles and think, "Where do I even go? Is there a place for me?" But remember, puzzles evolve. Maybe back in the day, the puzzle was just squares and circles, but now? Now, the puzzle's got to catch up with reality, which includes all sorts of shapes.

If you're a triangle, you're not a square missing a side. You're a complete, awesome triangle. If you're a star, you're not a circle with too many points. You're a brilliant, shining star. And if you're a shape that doesn't have a name yet, well, you're a trailblazer, making a new spot in the puzzle for others like you.

The real deal is this - you don't need to change it to fit the puzzle. The puzzle needs to change to fit you. And guess what? It's slowly happening. People are questioning the old slots, making new spaces, and realizing that different shapes bring their own cool vibes to the table. So embrace your shape, however it looks.

Because a puzzle with only one type of piece isn't just boring—it's incomplete. Your shape, whatever it is, makes the puzzle of life richer and fuller. So go ahead and claim your space. The puzzle's not complete without you.

This is super important for LGBTQIA+ folks who are figuring out what growing up means and learning to take responsibility for their own lives. Recognizing how society and culture have tried to shape your piece can help you understand why you might feel a certain way about your gender. You get to decide where your piece fits, not those invisible hands.

Understanding How Society And Culture

Understanding how society and culture have tried to mold your puzzle piece is like getting a map of the game board. This is key for LGBTQIA+ folks who are navigating the maze of growing up and taking on new responsibilities. You see, once you know where those invisible hands are coming from, you can start making your own decisions about where your piece fits rather than just getting pushed around.

Being LGBTQIA+ might mean your puzzle piece doesn't look like what most people expect, and that's okay. You're not just dealing with the "be tough" or "be nurturing" kinds of rules. You might also be tackling expectations about who you should love, how you should dress, or even what pronouns people should use for you. These are extra layers on your puzzle piece, extra expectations that you might feel like you have to meet.

How do you take responsibility for your own piece? It would help if you got to know it really well. Is it a triangle? A star? Something else entirely? Knowing your shape, its edges, and its curves helps you figure out where you want it to go. That's the 'Know Yourself' part of the LARK Code.

Stand Up For Your Piece.

If those invisible hands try to push you somewhere you don't want to go, it's okay to push back. That's the 'Respect Yourself' and 'Love Yourself' parts. You respect your piece enough to know it doesn't have to squeeze into a slot where it doesn't fit. And you love it enough to search for the right spot, even if it takes time.

Accepting that your piece is different can be tough, but it's also empowering. That's the 'Accept Yourself' bit. Once you realize your piece is supposed to be different—because every piece in a good puzzle is—you can stop worrying so much about those invisible hands and focus on where you feel you belong.

In the end, growing up LGBTQIA+ and taking responsibility means recognizing that you're the one who gets to place your puzzle piece. You choose where it fits best, how it connects with other pieces, and what picture it helps to create. It's your move, not the invisible hands. And you know what? That's where the real power lies—in choosing your spot in the puzzle and making it a better, more complete picture because you're a part of it.

The Gender Spectrum

Introduction To The Concept Of The Gender Spectrum.

When you're piecing together a puzzle, you usually start with an idea of what the final picture should look like, right? But what if someone told you that this puzzle doesn't have just one correct way to be completed? The idea might feel a bit weird, but it's also kinda freeing.

Imagine you're sitting down at a table, and in front of you is a big puzzle. Usually, there's a picture on the box that shows you what the finished puzzle should look like, right? You've got your corner pieces, your edge pieces, and everything in the middle that's supposed to fit just so to make that picture. But what if someone took away that box and said, "Hey, this puzzle can look like whatever you want it to look like. There's no one right way to do it."

That thought might make you scratch your head. We're so used to having guidelines, rules, or an example to follow. It's like someone just handed you a whole new set of puzzle pieces that you didn't even know could exist. You might even feel a bit overwhelmed, wondering where to start.

But then, the freedom of it starts to sink in. You realize you can create your own picture, something that's uniquely yours. It's like an art project and a puzzle in one. You don't have to follow someone else's idea of what's right or beautiful. And if you decide halfway through that, you want to change the picture? That's totally okay, too. You can rearrange the pieces, find new ones, or even toss some out that no longer fit. You have the freedom to change and evolve.

Understanding the Gender Spectrum is a lot like that. In the past, people were told that there were only two ways to be - male or female. It was as if everyone were handed a two-piece puzzle and told to make it fit, even if the pieces didn't match how they felt inside. But now, we're starting to realize that gender is a much more complex and beautiful picture. It's not just two pieces. It's many, many pieces that can be arranged in countless ways to reflect how you truly feel. Some people might have a puzzle that looks traditionally male or female, and that's totally fine. But for others, their puzzle might include a mix of pieces that represent being non-binary, genderqueer, or something else.

What's awesome about understanding the Gender Spectrum is that it gives you the tools and the language to build your own puzzle based on your own experiences and feelings. Remember, there's no time limit on this, and it's more than okay to ask for help or to look to others for inspiration.

Male And Female

You see, a lot of folks used to think that gender was like a really simple puzzle with just two - male and female. For a long time, people believed you had to fit snugly into one of these two categories based on the body you were born with. But over time, people started to realize that this two-piece puzzle was missing a whole bunch of pieces. It didn't capture the full, beautiful range of how people feel and identify themselves when it comes to gender.

One piece is labeled "male," and the other is labeled "female." For a long time, everyone thought that completing this puzzle was super easy. You're born, someone looks at you and decides which piece you are, and boom, your puzzle is done. It was like having a puzzle with only corners, no middle pieces. Simple, but not very exciting or true to life, right?

The idea that gender is either "male" or "female" based on physical traits is like saying a whole forest is just "trees" and "not-trees." It leaves out so much detail. What about the different types of trees, the animals that live there, or the rivers that flow through it? Similarly, the two-piece gender puzzle misses out on the rich variety of human experiences and identities.

People began to realize that there were folks who didn't fit neatly into those two pieces. Some felt like they were in between, floating around, or even far away from those two original pieces. It was like discovering that the puzzle actually had many extra pieces hiding in the box, and these pieces had different shapes, colors, and patterns. Some were labeled non-binary, genderfluid, or two-spirit, among others.

And guess what? Those pieces weren't actually "extra." They were essential for a lot of people to complete their own puzzles. Without these pieces, their puzzles felt incomplete or even wrong. People began to understand that forcing everyone into a two-piece puzzle wasn't just oversimplified. It was unfair and didn't reflect the reality of human experience.

The two-piece puzzle also didn't make room for personal growth or change. In a more complex puzzle, you can rearrange pieces as you find out more about yourself. Maybe a piece that fit when you were younger doesn't quite fit now. That's totally normal. A puzzle is allowed to be a work in progress, just like you.

As people became more aware and accepting of these different pieces, the concept of the Gender Spectrum started to make a lot more sense. It acknowledged that each person's puzzle is their own and can contain an array of pieces that make it unique, beautiful, and, most importantly, true to them.

That's the cool thing about expanding your understanding of gender beyond the basic two-piece puzzle. It's not just about adding more options. It's about acknowledging and celebrating the full range of human diversity. And when you do that, you're not just helping yourself get to know you better. You're making the world a more understanding and accepting place for everyone. Remember the LARK Code—Love, Accept, Respect, Know—and you'll be well on your way to completing your own unique puzzle.

Full Puzzle Box

The Gender Spectrum is like the full puzzle box, filled with an assortment of pieces that represent all the different ways people can be

male, female, both, neither, or something else entirely. There's a term for almost every feeling or identity you can think of. Have you heard of non-binary, genderqueer, or genderfluid? These are just some of the many pieces that fit into this expansive puzzle.

Think of the Gender Spectrum as a puzzle box that's filled to the brim with a wide variety of pieces. Do you know how some puzzle boxes have all kinds of colors, shapes, and intricate details? Well, that's how diverse the Gender Spectrum is. It's not a one-color, boring puzzle. It's a vibrant mix of pieces that come in all sorts of unique shapes and sizes.

Now, let's talk about some of these pieces. You've got your "male" and "female" pieces, which many people are familiar with. These are like the corner pieces of the puzzle. A lot of folks start with these because they're what society talks about the most. But remember, corner pieces only help you build the frame. They're not the entire puzzle.

Then you've got pieces like "non-binary," "genderqueer," and "genderfluid." If you haven't heard these terms before, no worries. These pieces help fill in the spaces that "male" and "female" don't cover. Someone who's non-binary doesn't strictly identify as just male or female. Their gender identity might float somewhere in between or outside those categories. Genderqueer is a term for people who reject traditional gender distinctions altogether, kind of like tossing out the old rulebook for how to solve a puzzle. And if you're genderfluid, your sense of gender might shift and change over time, like a puzzle piece that can fit in multiple places depending on how you feel.

But wait, there's more! Ever heard of "agender"? That's another piece. It's for people who feel they don't have a gender at all, like a blank puzzle piece that doesn't want to be colored in. And terms like "two-spirit" come from Indigenous cultures and represent another unique piece of the gender puzzle. The list goes on, with terms like "bigender," "demiboy," "demigirl," and so many more.

What's amazing is that there's a term, or a puzzle piece, for almost every feeling or identity you could think of. That means you have the freedom to explore and find the pieces that fit your puzzle perfectly, even if it takes some time to figure it out.

The more we acknowledge these different pieces, the better we get at understanding the full picture of human diversity. And as you're sorting through your own pieces, always keep the LARK Code in mind—Love, Accept, Respect, Know. That's your guide to making your puzzle a masterpiece that's unique to you.

Where Do These Extra Pieces Come From?

Well, science helps us understand a bit. Biology, like hormones and brain structure, gives us some of the foundational pieces. But remember, puzzles also have a lot of middle pieces, and those can come from your own personal feelings and experiences.

Imagine you've opened a puzzle box, and you've got all sorts of pieces scattered on the table. Some pieces you recognize right away. They're the basics, the foundational pieces that most people talk about. These are like the biological factors that shape gender—hormones, chromosomes, and brain structures. Scientists point to these as part of why people feel a certain way about their gender. These are kinda like the edge and corner pieces in a puzzle. They give you a starting frame but don't complete the picture.

Now, what about the middle pieces, the ones that add detail, color, and complexity to your puzzle? These can be likened to psychological and personal experiences. Think about the first time you felt different or the first time you felt a sense of "this is me" when thinking about your gender. These "aha" moments are like finding a puzzle piece that perfectly fits, helping you understand a bit more about the overall picture you're creating. Your feelings, how you see yourself, and how you relate to the world all contribute to these middle pieces.

Then there's your environment—your family, friends, the media, and even the laws and traditions where you live. All these external factors can offer up puzzle pieces, too, but here's the thing - you get to decide whether to place these pieces into your puzzle or not. Maybe your family always handed you "girl" pieces because you were assigned female at birth. Still, you've realized that those pieces don't actually fit your picture. You have the freedom to explore and find the pieces that truly fit you.

Sometimes, you might even reshape or color your puzzle pieces based on new experiences or deeper understanding. Let's say you've always felt like a "male" piece but then have experiences that make you realize you're more of a "non-binary" piece. That's absolutely okay. Puzzles can be rearranged, and people grow and change.

Where do these extra pieces come from? They come from a blend of biology, your personal feelings and experiences, and the world around you. Each source is like a smaller puzzle box within the bigger one, offering pieces that you can choose to add to your own unique masterpiece.

Society

You're busy sorting your puzzle pieces, right? And then along comes society, holding out pieces that they think should go in your puzzle. These pieces are shaped by all sorts of things—culture, traditions, and even the latest trends on social media. Think about those sayings you've heard like, "Boys don't cry," or "Girls should like pink." Those are society's pieces, ready-made and handed to you on a platter.

But here's where things get interesting - just because someone hands you a puzzle piece doesn't mean you have to use it. Imagine if someone tried to stick a piece from a totally different puzzle into yours. Would you try to jam it in, even if it doesn't fit? Probably not. Your puzzle is your own work of art, and you're the one who decides what goes into it.

Society's pieces can be pretty persuasive, though. They come with labels saying, "Most people use this piece" or "This piece is normal," and it can be tempting to try and make those pieces fit. Some people do manage to fit those pieces into their own puzzles and feel perfectly happy with them. And that's okay! But if you're looking at a piece and thinking, "Nah, this isn't me," you have every right to set it aside.

Even cooler? You can also modify these pieces. Maybe you take a "boys don't cry" piece and reshape it into "boys have feelings too." Or maybe you blend pieces together, creating a mix of traditionally "male" and "female" traits that feel right for you. The tools to shape, add, or even remove pieces are all in your hands.

And sometimes, setting aside or reshaping a societal piece is a big deal. It can feel like you're breaking the rules or going against the grain. And you know what? That's totally fine. In fact, it's more than fine—it's your right. Making your puzzle true to you might just help others feel brave enough to do the same with their puzzles.

The Gender Spectrum

The Gender Spectrum isn't an exclusive club. Think of it like a big puzzle table where everyone is welcome to come over, sort their pieces, and start building. Whether you identify as LGBTQIA+ or not, the table's open to you. Why? Because the Gender Spectrum isn't just about individual puzzles. It's about understanding the massive, intricate, and beautiful jigsaw that humanity as a whole creates.

Learning about the Gender Spectrum helps you understand why some people have puzzles that look very different from yours. Imagine you've always thought puzzles only come in landscapes, but then you see someone working on an abstract design or a cosmic scene. Your first thought might be, "Hey, that's not what a puzzle is supposed to be!" But once you know about the Gender Spectrum, you're more like, "Whoa, cool puzzle. Never thought of it that way!"

And let's face it, respecting other people's puzzles makes life a lot easier and way more interesting. If everyone's trying to force their pieces into one or two cookie-cutter puzzles, things will get dull pretty fast. But when you see the incredible variety of puzzles people can create using the Gender Spectrum, life becomes a lot more colorful and exciting. It's like walking into an art gallery where every work is unique and fascinating in its own way.

Plus, understanding other people's puzzles can help you with your own. Maybe you've been trying to jam a piece into your puzzle because you thought it was the only option. Seeing how someone else has arranged their pieces might give you ideas for your own. It's like swapping puzzle strategies without even having to move a piece.

The Gender Spectrum can also help reduce misunderstandings and conflict. Think about how much easier it is to respect someone's space, choices, and identity when you get where they're coming from. It's like if someone's working on a puzzle next to you and you understand why they've chosen certain pieces, you're less likely to bump into their table or mess up their work.

The Gender Spectrum isn't just a tool for self-discovery. It's also a blueprint for understanding and respecting others. No matter who you are or how you identify, taking a seat at this puzzle table can give you a richer, more empathetic view of the world. Do you know how a blueprint is a detailed plan for a building? Well, the Gender Spectrum acts like a blueprint, but not just for one person. It's like a master plan that can guide everyone in understanding the intricate architecture of human identity. Just like a good blueprint helps builders avoid mistakes and understand the bigger picture, the Gender Spectrum helps us navigate the complex world of gender identity without stepping on toes or making assumptions.

When you sit down at this metaphorical puzzle table that is the Gender Spectrum, you're not just working on your own puzzle—you're also gaining the tools to understand everyone else's. Think of it like this.

If your friend is working on a super tricky 3D puzzle, and you've only ever done flat 2D puzzles, you might be puzzled (pun intended!) at first. But once you know that 3D puzzles exist and how they work, you're not just like, "Ah, I get it," you're also more likely to appreciate the skill it takes to put that 3D puzzle together.

Taking a seat at the Gender Spectrum table makes you more empathetic because it helps you "get" where people are coming from. It's like gaining puzzle superpowers. You can look at many pieces and start to understand how they might fit into someone else's picture, not just your own. This empathy isn't just good vibes. It's practical. When you understand someone else's puzzle, you're less likely to make snap judgments or say stuff that might accidentally hurt them.

And let's talk about this "richer view of the world" part. Before knowing about the Gender Spectrum, you might see the world in black and white—or, in this case, just male and female. But understanding the spectrum is like suddenly seeing it in full color. You realize there's a whole rainbow of identities and experiences out there, and that makes your view of the world richer, more nuanced, and way more interesting. It's like upgrading from a basic puzzle with big, chunky pieces to one with intricate details and colors that make the final picture something you could stare at for hours.

Yeah, sitting down at the Gender Spectrum puzzle table isn't just an inward journey. It's also like putting on a pair of super cool, empathy-boosting glasses that let you see the intricate details in everyone else's puzzles, too. And the more people understand and respect each other's unique puzzles, the more awesome the world becomes for everyone. And as you build your own puzzle, guided by your trusty LARK Code, you'll be making it easier for others to do the same. Because, at the end of the day, each unique puzzle contributes to the big, amazing mosaic that is human diversity.

Whenever you hear someone talk about the Gender Spectrum, just think about a puzzle that you're putting together piece by piece. Some pieces you're born with, some you discover along the way, and some you might toss out because they don't fit anymore. And that's totally fine. Just remember the LARK Code, and keep on puzzling.

Non-Binary, Genderqueer, And Other Gender Identities

"non-binary." If you think about a traditional puzzle of a sunset, you might have one side that's all bright and sunny and another that's dark and night-time, right? Well, some people realized their puzzle isn't just day or night. It's that amazing moment of twilight, the in-between. That's what being non-binary is like. It's saying, "Hey, I don't fit neatly into the 'male' or 'female' boxes. I'm something else, something that breaks the mold."

Imagine you're working on that sunset puzzle, right? Most folks might think there are just two main parts - the bright, sunny day and the dark, quiet night. But if you've ever looked at the sky during twilight, you know that's where some of the most magical colors happen. We're talking purples, pinks, blues, and even some colors you can't easily name. That's the beauty of twilight. It's complex and doesn't fit into a simple "day or night" box.

In this analogy, being non-binary is like embracing the twilight in your puzzle. It's about recognizing that gender isn't just this or that but a whole range of experiences and feelings that can blend together in unexpected ways. Being non-binary means that you don't feel strictly male or strictly female, or maybe you feel a bit of both, or maybe it varies. The key here is the freedom to be who you genuinely are, not just picking a predefined box and trying to cram yourself into it.

When someone identifies as non-binary, they're taking a stand against the old-school way of looking at gender. They're saying, "Nope, I'm not going to let society tell me that there are only two ways to be. My puzzle is going to include the whole sky, twilight and all." They might use different pronouns like "they/them" or maybe stick with "he" or "she" but redefine what that means for them. The important thing is that they're defining their own identity on their own terms.

Being non-binary can feel liberating. Imagine if someone told you that you could only use blue and pink pieces in your puzzle. You'd miss out on so many other beautiful colors! When you identify as non-binary, it's like suddenly having access to a whole new set of puzzle pieces with colors and shapes you never thought were allowed but make your puzzle truly one-of-a-kind.

And just like twilight can look different depending on where you are or what the weather's like, being non-binary can mean different things to different people. That's the magic of it. It's a flexible, inclusive way to understand gender. It's not about fitting into an existing mold. It's about creating your own unique space in the world, a space that lets you be you.

Genderqueer

Imagine you've got a table full of puzzle pieces from all sorts of different sets—a slice of pizza from a food-themed puzzle, a spaceship from a sci-fi set, and a cute puppy from a pet puzzle. Now, someone who's sticking to just one traditional puzzle might look over and think, "What's going on here? Those pieces don't belong together!" But you know better. You know that combining all these different pieces can create a picture that's entirely new, entirely unique, and entirely you.

Being genderqueer is kind of like embracing the idea that your puzzle doesn't have to come from just one box. You're not limited to the standard-issue "male" or "female" sets. you can pull from multiple places to express who you are. It's like saying, "I'm gonna grab this slice of pizza, this spaceship, and this puppy, and guess what? They all fit in my puzzle because my puzzle is a reflection of me, not someone else's idea of what a puzzle should be."

And the awesome thing is, being genderqueer isn't just about rejecting old labels. it's about creating new possibilities. Each different piece you add—whether it's the way you dress, the pronouns you use, or how you feel inside—adds a new layer to your identity. You're making something richer and more complex than any single puzzle could ever be.

Just like each piece from a different puzzle brings its own unique shape and color, each aspect of your gender identity brings something special to the table. Maybe you feel masculine some days and feminine on others. Or maybe you've got this constant blend going on that doesn't fit neatly into either of those categories. That's the beauty of being genderqueer. it's fluid, flexible, and totally individual to you.

Remember, your puzzle doesn't have to look like anyone else's to be valid. The whole point is that it's yours. You get to decide what pieces fit, which ones you want to include, and how you want to arrange them. And just like a multi-themed puzzle becomes a conversation piece that gets people talking and asking questions, being genderqueer often sparks conversations that help break down old stereotypes and open up new ways of understanding gender. And who knows? Your unique puzzle might just inspire someone else to start building their own, one that's just as unique and beautiful as yours.

Genderfluid," "Agender," "Two-Spirit," And So Many More

Let's zoom in on "genderfluid" as another piece of the puzzle—or, more accurately, as a puzzle that keeps changing its shape. You know those puzzles that have multiple solutions, where you can rearrange the pieces to make entirely different pictures? That's a lot like being genderfluid. One day, your puzzle might look like a beautiful garden filled with flowers, and then it could be a bustling cityscape. And that's not because you're indecisive. It's because your sense of gender is dynamic. It's like you've got this living, breathing artwork that represents who you are, and it changes to match how you're feeling.

When you're genderfluid, there's no need to commit to a single, permanent layout for your puzzle. You might feel more masculine some days, more feminine in others, or maybe something entirely different. And guess what? All of those arrangements are equally awesome and equally you. Your puzzle, your rules.

Imagine the freedom of not having to say, "This is the one and only way my puzzle should look." It's liberating, right? You get to explore different parts of yourself on different days or even at different times of the day. This fluidity can also open your eyes to how limited traditional ideas of gender can be. I mean, why stick to one picture on the box when you've got a whole gallery of images inside you, waiting to be assembled and appreciated?

But wait, there's more! Other puzzle pieces like "agender" and "two-spirit" offer more layers to explore. For example, being agender is like saying, "You know what? My puzzle doesn't need to have any of those traditional gender pieces. I'm perfectly complete without them." On the other hand, "two-spirit" is a term that comes from some Indigenous cultures in North America and can mean that you embody both masculine and feminine spirits. It's like having a puzzle that merges two different but complementary pictures into one.

There's a whole universe of gender identities out there, each adding its unique shape, color, and texture to the vast landscape of human experience. Whether you're piecing together your own identity or trying to understand someone else's, it's crucial to remember that every puzzle is valid, every puzzle is different, and every puzzle enriches the world in its own way.

Agender

Let's delve into "agender" a bit more. Picture this - You've got a puzzle in front of you. Instead of filling it with various elements like mountains, rivers, or buildings, you opt for a clear, endless sky. No distractions, just open space. It's complete in its simplicity and serene in its openness.

Being agender is a lot like that—choosing the sky-only puzzle. It's not that you're missing anything. It's that you've found completeness in not assigning any specific gender to yourself. It's a way of saying, "Hey, this concept of gender? It doesn't define who I am. I'm just me." Some people might think a sky with no sun or moon is empty, but you know better. That sky is full of air, full of potential, full of life—even if you can't see it with the naked eye.

Now, this doesn't mean you're against the idea of gender or that you don't 'get it.' Nah, you get it just fine. It's just that, for you, gender isn't a necessary part of your self-portrait. Your puzzle is complete without those traditional pieces that say "male" or "female" or anything in between. It's not an absence. It's the presence of something else, something that can't be easily categorized but is no less real or valid.

It's important to remember that being agender isn't the same for everyone, just like no two clear skies are alike. Some people might feel a sense of neutrality like they're hovering in the middle of the gender spectrum but not really landing on any particular point. Others might feel a total disconnect from the concept of gender altogether. And that's cool! Your sky can be dawn, high noon, twilight, or midnight. It's still the sky, and it's still your puzzle.

By understanding terms like agender, we get closer to seeing the full picture of what human diversity looks like. It's like gathering around a big table full of puzzle pieces and realizing that there are infinite ways to create something meaningful and beautiful. And the coolest part? You get to decide what your sky looks like, no one else.

You Get To Decide Where They Fit

When you're assembling a puzzle, you're both the artist and the puzzle master. You're in control of how the pieces fit together, and sometimes, you even get to decide what those pieces are. Isn't that awesome?

Let's say you have all these unique puzzle pieces, like non-binary, genderqueer, genderfluid, and agender. Each of these pieces has its own shape, color, and vibe. Non-binary might be that cool shade of twilight blue that adds depth to your sky. Genderqueer could be a splash of rainbow colors that make your puzzle pop. Genderfluid is like the swirl of changing hues that gives your puzzle a dynamic, ever-changing look. And agender? That might be the open sky that brings a sense of peaceful balance to the whole picture.

The thing is, you don't have to use every piece you come across. Maybe today, you feel like adding the genderfluid piece because it just fits. Tomorrow, you might take it out and put it in the non-binary piece instead. Or heck, you might decide that today is a sky-only day, focusing on the agender aspect. You get to choose.

And get this - your puzzle isn't just for you. When other people see it, they can learn something, too. Maybe your use of the non-binary piece helps someone else realize that it's okay not to fit neatly into a box. Or your beautiful, sky-only agender layout could help someone see that gender doesn't have to be the defining aspect of who they are.

Bottom line? You're not just building a puzzle. You're creating a work of art that's as unique as you are. And just like any artist, you have the freedom to decide what materials you want to work with, how they should be arranged, and what your final masterpiece looks like. So go ahead, be both the artist and the puzzle master of your life. Take those special pieces—whether they're non-binary, genderqueer, genderfluid, agender, or something else—and make something amazing. Remember your puzzle and your rules.

As you keep working on your puzzle, don't be afraid to explore these unique pieces. They're what make your puzzle truly yours, and understanding them can also help you appreciate the cool, one-of-a-kind puzzles that other people are working on, too.

Celebrating The Diversity Of Gender Expressions

Totally! Let's imagine a massive puzzle party where everyone's invited. The tables are lined up with a zillion different puzzles, each one representing a unique person from the LGBTQIA+ community. When you walk through this room, what's the first thing you notice? The incredible diversity, right? There are puzzles with splashes of color, some that are black and white, some with intricate details, and some that are beautifully simple.

Walking into this massive puzzle party is like stepping into a wonderland of self-expression. You can almost feel the energy in the room, buzzing from table to table. As you wander through, the first thing that hits you is how different each puzzle is—yet they're all connected by being part of this awesome celebration of the LGBTQIA+ community.

Imagine stopping at the first table and seeing a puzzle bursting with vibrant colors and complex patterns. It's almost like stepping into a carnival. It's full of life and impossible to ignore. This puzzle might represent someone who identifies as genderqueer and celebrates that through an array of colorful clothing and dynamic self-expression.

You walk over to a puzzle that's stunning in its simplicity. It's almost entirely shades of blue, creating a sense of calm and peace. This could represent someone who identifies as agender, someone who finds comfort in shedding societal expectations about what gender should look like.

Now, you move to another table where you find a puzzle that's different every time you look at it. One moment, it's a roaring ocean wave. The next, it's a serene beach scene. This ever-changing puzzle could symbolize someone who identifies as genderfluid, constantly exploring and redefining their own understanding of gender.

As you stroll further, you notice a black-and-white puzzle. At first glance, it might look straightforward, but as you get closer, you notice intricate details and subtle shades of grey. This could be someone who identifies as non-binary, blending elements typically associated with both men and women but fitting neatly into neither category.

And you can't forget the tables that have multiple puzzles going on at the same time, side by side, all connected in some way. These might represent individuals who identify with multiple gender expressions or identities—maybe they're bigender or two-spirit.

What's incredible about this puzzle party is that each table you visit, each puzzle you examine, teaches you something new—not just about the person it represents but also about the richness of the human experience. These puzzles aren't just for show. They're educational tools that help everyone understand the broad scope of what it means to be human and to have a gender identity.

And remember, this room is open to everyone. Whether you're part of the LGBTQIA+ community or an ally, there's a spot for you at one of these tables. Even if your puzzle is still a work in progress, that's okay. The beauty of this massive puzzle party is that everyone's invited to contribute their uniqueness to this incredible tapestry of human diversity.

Diversity In Gender Expression Is Something To Celebrate

diversity in the LGBTQIA+ community isn't just a fact. it's a celebration, a party that everyone's invited to. Imagine walking into this big room filled with puzzles and feeling like you're surrounded by art galleries, each one dedicated to someone's life and experiences. It's not just an exhibit. it's a chorus of voices, each singing their own unique tune.

The genderqueer puzzle, with its vibrant colors, is like the life of the party. Imagine if that puzzle could talk—it would probably be full of stories about defying expectations and embracing a mix of characteristics that society traditionally thinks of as 'male' or 'female.' It's like a burst of fireworks in puzzle form, sparking conversations and catching everyone's attention.

Right next to it, the agender puzzle brings in a sense of serenity. Its calming shades invite people to take a deep breath and think more deeply about what gender means. The puzzle's simple hues and peaceful design show that sometimes less is more. For some, shedding the labels and just being is a way to find peace. It's like the quiet corner at a party where you can go to have a real heart-to-heart with someone.

Now, let's not forget the genderfluid puzzle. This one's like the chameleon of the room, always adapting and changing. If you watched it for an entire day, you might see it rearrange itself into different themes or settings. That's what makes it so fascinating—it refuses to be pinned down, teaching everyone that it's okay to be in flux, to be a work in progress.

Then you've got the non-binary puzzles, disrupting the idea that puzzles have to be two-sided or fit into predetermined categories. These puzzles may have pieces that could fit into multiple other puzzles. Still, they come together to create something totally unique. They're like the DJs at the party, mixing different beats to create a whole new sound that makes everyone stop and listen.

What's special about this diverse room is that every puzzle belongs, and each one adds something valuable. Whether you're adding vibrant splashes of color, peaceful pockets of simplicity, dynamic transformations, or revolutionary remixes, your puzzle has a spot in this room.

And here's another thing

having all these different puzzles side by side doesn't just make the room more interesting. It also makes it more inclusive. When you see such a wide range of expressions and identities, it sends a powerful message - whoever you are, however you identify, there's room for you here. And not just room to exist but to be celebrated, explored, and understood. That's what makes this party so unforgettable.

Two-Spirit, Bigender, And A Host Of Other Terms T

Let's not forget about the other puzzles that add even more layers to this amazing collection. Think about the two-spirit puzzle, for example. This puzzle has roots that go deep, drawing from Indigenous cultures and understandings of gender. It's like the antique piece at the party, full of history and stories that most modern puzzles might not have. It's a connector between past and present, teaching us that understanding gender in diverse ways isn't a new thing. It's been around for centuries.

Then you have the bigender puzzle, and boy, is it a mind-bender! Imagine a puzzle that's one picture on one side and a totally different picture on the other. It's like those optical illusions where you see a vase one moment, and two faces the next. The bigender puzzle reminds us that some people feel a strong connection to both 'male' and 'female' identities. And because it holds two pictures in one, it's a great conversation starter about how complex and multifaceted gender can be.

And let's not forget the other terms that even some adults haven't heard of—like demiboy, demigirl, and gender questioning. These are like the indie puzzles at the party. Maybe they aren't as well-known, but they have their unique charm and a niche following. Each of these identities, represented by its own unique puzzles, adds a new texture, a new splash of color, or an intricate detail that makes you want to lean in closer to understand what it's all about.

The thing is, each puzzle has its own world inside it—a unique experience, a one-of-a-kind expression of someone's life and feelings. It's like each one is its own mini-universe of shapes, colors, and stories. They might share a table, but don't be fooled. Each puzzle is a realm unto itself.

When you step back and look at this room filled with puzzles, you're not just seeing pieces of cardboard. You're seeing slices of life, snippets of stories, and flashes of feelings. Each one makes the room richer, fuller, and more intriguing. And you know what? Every time someone adds a new puzzle to the table, it's like the room grows a little bit bigger, making space for even more experiences and expressions to be celebrated.

Celebrating Diversity

It's more than just making the room look like a rainbow of experiences. it's about making the room feel like home to everyone who walks in. Imagine if you had a puzzle that you were kind of unsure about—maybe it has a mix of pieces that you think don't traditionally go together. But then you see many other puzzles doing their own mix-and-match thing, and suddenly, you're not Worried about whether your pieces fit the "right" way. You start to feel like your puzzle is another brushstroke in this huge, complex masterpiece.

And that green light you're talking about? It's not just saying, "Hey, you're welcome here." It's saying, "Hey, you belong here." When people see that they can bring their authentic selves to the table, it encourages them to do just that. They start adding their own pieces to the mix, making the room even more diverse and inclusive. And the more people feel they can be themselves, the more they'll want to learn about others' experiences too. It's a win-win, really.

The more we celebrate this diversity of puzzles—of gender identities—the better we get at welcoming everyone, no matter their shape, color, or pattern.

And the more we get to know each other's puzzles, the better we understand that everyone has their unique place in this room, on this table, in this world.

Looking At Other People's Puzzles

Imagine you're at this big puzzle party, and you see someone placing a piece that's got this super cool design you've never seen before. It clicks something in your mind. You think, "Whoa, I didn't even know that piece could exist, but it makes total sense for my puzzle too!"

Seeing that diversity around you is like having a light bulb go off in your head. It sparks ideas and new ways of thinking about your own puzzle that you might not have come up with on your own. You get to be like, "Hey, maybe I've been sticking to blues and greens, but what about adding some vibrant reds and yellows?" Or, "I never thought about mixing big pieces with small ones, but look how awesome it looks in that person's puzzle."

Yeah, diversity isn't just a showcase. It's a learning opportunity. You get to pick up little gems of wisdom as you walk through that room, and you might even change your puzzle a bit as you go along. And that's perfectly okay! Puzzles are meant to be rearranged, expanded, and even reimagined.

And here's the big-picture view

the more you learn, the more you grow. The more you grow, the more accepting you become—not just of others but of yourself. You start realizing that every puzzle piece, whether in your puzzle or someone else's, brings value to the table. That mindset is like a ripple in a pond. It starts with you but spreads out, making the whole room—heck, maybe even the whole world—a better, more accepting place.

The next time you think about the LGBTQIA+ community, remember that giant puzzle party. Each person brings their own masterpiece, and each masterpiece adds something special to the room. It's not just about celebrating these puzzles. It's about appreciating what each one brings to the table.

Navigating the Maze of Challenges

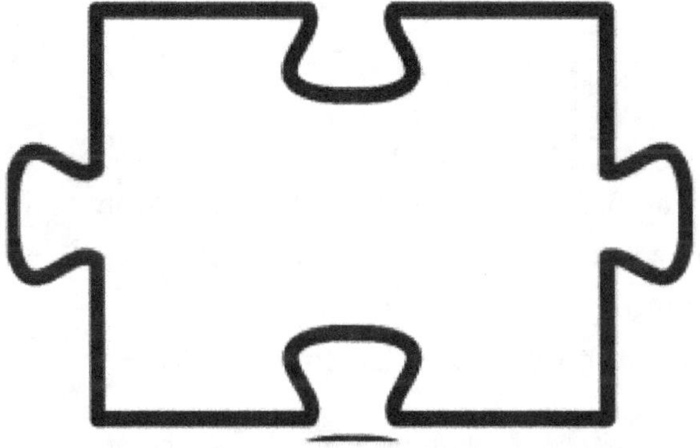

In the vast puzzle of life, individuals within the LGBTQIA+ community often find themselves navigating through a complex maze filled with challenges and obstacles. These challenges can arise from various sources, including societal norms, legal barriers, and personal interactions. Understanding and addressing these challenges is crucial in creating a more inclusive and supportive environment for all.

The Walls Of Discrimination

Imagine the walls of discrimination towering around you, forming barriers that obstruct your path at every turn. Discrimination against LGBTQIA+ individuals can manifest in many forms, including prejudice, stereotypes, and exclusion. These walls can make it difficult for individuals to express their true selves openly and without fear of judgment or reprisal.

Facing Legal Hurdles

In some parts of the world, discriminatory laws and policies further complicate the journey for LGBTQIA+ individuals. These legal hurdles can restrict access to basic rights such as marriage, adoption, and employment protections. Navigating a legal landscape that fails to recognize and protect LGBTQIA+ rights adds another layer of complexity to the puzzle of life.

Healthcare Challenges

Accessing healthcare can also present challenges for individuals within the LGBTQIA+ community. From discrimination by healthcare providers to a lack of culturally competent care, navigating the healthcare system can be daunting. These challenges can have serious implications for the physical and mental well-being of LGBTQIA+ individuals.

Family And Social Dynamics

For many, family and social support are essential pieces of the puzzle. However, coming out to family members and friends can be fraught with uncertainty and fear of rejection. The puzzle of navigating relationships with loved ones while staying true to oneself requires courage and resilience.

Intersectional Identities

Each individual's puzzle is unique, shaped not only by their LGBTQIA+ identity but also by other aspects of who they are, such as race, ethnicity, and socioeconomic status. Intersectionality adds layers of complexity to the challenges faced by LGBTQIA+ individuals, highlighting the importance of recognizing and addressing the interconnected systems of oppression they may encounter.

Resilience And Advocacy

Despite the challenges they face, LGBTQIA+ individuals demonstrate remarkable resilience and strength. Through advocacy, community support, and personal empowerment, they work to dismantle barriers and create a more inclusive society. Each step forward in the journey brings us closer to solving the puzzle of discrimination and building a world where everyone can live authentically and without fear.

Microaggressions And Everyday Challenges

In the intricate mosaic of life, LGBTQIA+ individuals often encounter subtle yet pervasive forms of discrimination known as microaggressions. These small but impactful acts can include insensitive remarks, invalidation of identities, and assumptions about gender and sexuality. Navigating these everyday challenges requires resilience and self-awareness, as well as allies who are willing to confront and challenge discriminatory behavior.

Religious And Cultural Obstacles

For many LGBTQIA+ individuals, religious and cultural beliefs can present significant barriers to acceptance and inclusion. The clash between personal identity and societal expectations rooted in religious or cultural norms can create inner turmoil and external conflict. Navigating these complex intersections requires empathy, understanding, and a willingness to engage in dialogue that respects both individual identities and cultural traditions.

Bullying And Harassment

In the tapestry of social interactions, LGBTQIA+ individuals may face bullying, harassment, and violence simply for being who they are. From schoolyard taunts to workplace discrimination, the threat of physical and emotional harm looms large for many within the community. Addressing bullying and harassment requires proactive measures to create safe and supportive environments where all individuals can thrive without fear of persecution.

Legal Battles For Equality

In the legal landscape of society, LGBTQIA+ individuals and their allies have long fought battles for equal rights and protections under the law. From landmark court cases to grassroots activism, the struggle for LGBTQIA+ rights has been ongoing and hard-fought. Navigating the complexities of legal advocacy requires strategic thinking, perseverance, and a commitment to justice for all.

Intersectionality And Multiple Marginalizations

Within the intricate web of identities, LGBTQIA+ individuals often experience intersecting forms of oppression based on factors such as race, ethnicity, disability, and immigration status. These multiple marginalizations can compound the challenges faced by individuals within the community, amplifying the impact of discrimination and exclusion. Recognizing and addressing intersectionality is essential for creating inclusive spaces that honor the diverse experiences and identities of LGBTQIA+ individuals.

Building Resilience And Community Support

Despite the myriad challenges they face, LGBTQIA+ individuals demonstrate resilience and strength in the face of adversity. Through community support networks, mentorship, and self-care practices, individuals within the community find strength in solidarity and connection. Navigating the complexities of discrimination requires resilience, resourcefulness, and a commitment to supporting one another on the journey toward equality and justice.

As we continue to unravel the complexities of the puzzle, let us remember that addressing the challenges faced by LGBTQIA+ individuals requires collective effort and unwavering commitment to equality and justice. Together, we can create a world where everyone's puzzle pieces fit together harmoniously, regardless of their gender identity or sexual orientation.

Addressing The Challenges And Discrimination

Facing challenges and discrimination as someone in the LGBTQIA+ community is like working on your puzzle in a room where some people don't want you to complete it—or even start it in the first place. It's like they're throwing their own ideas of what your puzzle should be right on top of yours, making it harder to see your picture clearly. Some might try to mess up your progress by taking pieces away or even hiding them.

When you're in the LGBTQIA+ community and trying to put together your own puzzle, it's like some people keep reaching over and messing with your pieces. Imagine you're focused on making good progress. Then, someone comes over and flips the table, scattering your puzzle pieces everywhere. That's how it can feel when you face challenges and discrimination. It's frustrating and disheartening, and it interrupts the work you're doing to understand and be yourself.

In some cases, people might even go so far as to steal some of your puzzle pieces. Let's say you finally found a piece that represents your true identity, something you're excited about. But then someone tries to take it away, saying it doesn't belong or that it's wrong somehow. That can be a pretty big blow, like when you're denied rights or opportunities because of your gender identity—like jobs, housing, or even using a public restroom that aligns with who you are.

Or think about those folks who throw their own puzzle pieces onto your board. These are the people who insist on using the wrong pronouns for you or reject your identity because it doesn't fit their beliefs. It's as if they're trying to force their own puzzle pieces into your masterpiece, not caring if it messes up the image you've been working so hard to create.

Sometimes, the people messing with your puzzle are even close to you—like family or friends who just don't get it. That hurts a lot because these are people you'd hope would be helping you find where your pieces go, not throwing extra, mismatched ones onto your board.

But here's something to remember - Your puzzle is yours and yours alone. You get to decide where each piece goes. You decide what the finished picture looks like, even if it's different from everyone else's. Indeed, you can't control other people messing with your puzzle, but you can choose how to react. Maybe you build a little fence around your puzzle, like setting boundaries. Maybe you find a community of people who are also building their own unique puzzles, and you look out for each other. These allies can help you find your scattered pieces and put them back where they belong.

In the end, the challenges and discrimination are like obstacles in your puzzle-building journey. They're tough, no doubt about it. Still, they're also opportunities for you to prove to yourself—and the world—that your puzzle is worth completing, no matter what anyone else says.

Misunderstanding Or Lack Of Knowledge

When you're building your puzzle of self-identity, misunderstanding or lack of knowledge from others can feel like someone tossing random pieces onto your table. Imagine you're diligently working, and then someone comes by and drops a piece featuring a dinosaur right onto your landscape scene. It's like when someone says, "Have you tried not being this way?" or "It's just a phase." Those comments are like that out-of-place dinosaur piece they don't fit and can really mess with your focus.

It's frustrating when people don't understand and offer up these mismatched puzzle pieces. These pieces aren't just wrong. They can also make you second-guess yourself. You might find yourself pausing and wondering, "Do I actually need this dinosaur piece in my landscape? Is something wrong with my picture?" It's a confusing and distracting moment, and sometimes, it can even make you feel like you're the one who's got it all wrong.

What can you do? Education is a game-changer. When people toss in these misplaced pieces because they don't know any better, sometimes showing them the correct placement—or that their piece doesn't belong on your board at all—can be enlightening. Of course, this is only if you feel safe and comfortable doing so. It's not your job to educate everyone. But suppose you decide to go that route. In that case, you might share resources, stories, or even parts of your own experience to help them understand that their dinosaur piece belongs to a whole different puzzle, not yours.

Sometimes, after a little education, these folks will stop tossing mismatched pieces your way. Instead, they might even start helping you find pieces that do fit, becoming allies instead of hindrances. And that's how you turn a challenge into an opportunity, clearing up misunderstandings one puzzle piece at a time.

Systemic Discrimination

Systemic discrimination isn't just an errant puzzle piece. It's like a whole set of rules that say only specific puzzles are allowed to be completed. Imagine you're in a puzzle-building contest, and suddenly, the judge says, "Sorry, we're only accepting landscape puzzles today. If you're working on anything else, you're disqualified." That's the weight and scope of systemic discrimination—it takes the issue to a whole other level, far beyond just individual misunderstandings.

How do you tackle something this big? Well, this is where teamwork really shines. You've got to get all the other puzzle builders who believe in diversity and freedom to join you. Together, you all can say, "This isn't fair. Every puzzle should get a chance to be built, admired, and celebrated."

Being part of a community working toward the same goal amplifies your voice. Activism can look like a lot of things. Maybe you join a march, attend meetings, or get involved with organizations that are fighting these bigger battles. It's like pooling all your extra puzzle pieces together to create something powerful and vivid that can't be ignored.

Voting is another way to make an impact. By casting your ballot, you're essentially voting for a world where all kinds of puzzles can exist. You're voting for judges who appreciate all kinds of puzzles, not just the landscapes. You're voting for rules that give everyone a fair shot at completing their own unique picture.

Donating to or volunteering with organizations that fight for LGBTQIA+ rights is like contributing to a community puzzle fund. Your time or money helps gather more pieces, fill in the gaps, and build a more inclusive and accepting world.

The fight against systemic discrimination is a group project. One person can't topple it alone, but a community of determined puzzle builders? Now that's a force to be reckoned with. Together, you can create a space where every puzzle is valued, and every person can build freely.

Personal Prejudice

Personal prejudice is like having someone walk right up to your table and start flipping your puzzle pieces onto the floor. They're not just clueless or misinformed. They're actively trying to mess up your work. In a situation like this, the most important thing is to protect yourself and your puzzle.

What do you do when someone tries to rip apart your hard work? Safety is a must. Sometimes, the best thing is to move your puzzle to a safer spot, away from anyone looking to tear it apart. This could mean physically leaving a place or situation or blocking someone online who's causing harm.

Reach out for help, too. Imagine a whole team of puzzle protectors standing beside you, ready to step in when things get tough. This team might include trusted friends and family members. Still, it could also consist of professionals or organizations designed to help. There are hotlines you can call, counselors who specialize in LGBTQIA+ issues, and even online communities full of people who've faced similar challenges.

Joining a supportive group or organization is like adding extra hands to help you guard your puzzle. And sometimes, when you're facing personal prejudice, there's strength in numbers. The more people you have supporting you, the harder it becomes for anyone to mess with your puzzle.

Not only can these groups offer emotional support, but they can also provide practical advice on how to deal with prejudice, discrimination, or even legal troubles. It's like getting tips and tricks on how to make your puzzle-building process smoother, more enjoyable, and safer for you.

Remember, it's okay to ask for help. Your puzzle is your own, but you don't have to build it entirely by yourself, especially when others are trying to take it apart. The goal is to create a masterpiece that's truly yours, and sometimes, that means leaning on others to help you protect it and make it shine.

Microaggressions

Microaggressions are those sneaky, little disruptions that can be easy to overlook but still mess up your puzzle. They're like tiny bumps to your table that scatter a few pieces here and there. One bump might not seem like a big deal, but imagine getting bumped over and over again. It can get really annoying and even make it tough to see your puzzle clearly.

How do you deal with these bumps? Well, the approach can vary. Sometimes, a quick "Hey, you're jostling the table" can make the person realize what they're doing and be more careful. It's like giving them a gentle reminder to watch their step around your puzzle.

But not everyone gets it with just a nudge. Some people don't even realize they're bumping the table. For those folks, you might need to have a more in-depth conversation. This could mean explaining why their actions, even if not mean-spirited, are messing up your work. It's like taking a minute to show them how every bump scatters your pieces, making it harder for you to complete your puzzle.

And hey, it's important to pick your battles. You might not have the energy to address every single bump, and that's okay. Some days, you might just want to focus on your puzzle and not worry about educating everyone who walks by. And that's totally fine. It's your puzzle, after all, and you get to decide how much time you spend on these bumps.

Dealing with microaggressions can be exhausting, but it's part of navigating a world where not everyone understands or respects your puzzle. The key is to find a balance that lets you protect your work and educate others without draining all your energy. After all, you've got a beautiful, unique puzzle to complete, and that's what really matters.

Each Challenge Is A Hurdle

Your puzzle is like your personal masterpiece, and just like any great work of art, it's worth protecting and nurturing. Yeah, challenges are like hurdles you have to jump over. Some are low, and some are high, but each one you clear makes you better at this puzzle-building game called life.

Let's not forget, though, that you're not doing this puzzle solo. For every person who nudges your table or tries to force in a piece that doesn't belong, there's someone else who gets it. These are the folks who look at your half-completed puzzle and see its potential. They might even have that missing edge piece you've been searching for. These are your allies, your cheerleaders, your fellow puzzle enthusiasts. Stick close to them because they make the journey a lot more fun and a bit easier.

When you're down or feeling like the hurdles are too high, these are the people who remind you to look at the big picture—your picture. They help you remember that every piece, every challenge, and every triumph is part of who you are. And when you finally slot in that last piece, they'll be right there cheering you on.

You'll face challenges, but you'll also collect wins along the way. Those wins, big or small, are moments to celebrate because they bring you one step closer to completing your puzzle. Every piece you successfully fit brings your picture into sharper focus. With each challenge you overcome, you become more of a puzzle master. Keep at it. Your unique, intricate, beautiful puzzle is worth every bit of effort you put into it.

Strategies For Coping With Prejudice And Fostering Resilience.

Coping with prejudice and building resilience is kind of like having a toolkit ready when you sit down to work on your puzzle. You've got to have strategies, not just for the puzzle but for dealing with the people who might want to mess it up. What can you put in that toolkit?

Expanding your toolkit for coping with prejudice and building resilience is like assembling a special set of tools just for puzzle-making. You want to make sure you're well-equipped for any situation—whether it's someone trying to mess with your puzzle or just getting stuck on a tricky section. What's gonna be in this super-duper toolkit?

Emotional Flashlight.

Imagine you're trying to find a specific piece, and the room's too dark. This tool helps you examine your own feelings and reactions. When someone says something hurtful, the "Emotional Flashlight" helps you pause and think,

"Why did that bother me? What's the best way to address this?" It's about understanding yourself so you can better handle what comes your way.

Ah, the "Emotional Flashlight" is a real game-changer. Imagine you're hunched over your puzzle, and you just can't figure out where this one tricky piece goes. The room's dim, and you're squinting, getting more and more frustrated. Then, you flip on your "Emotional Flashlight," and suddenly, you can see not just the puzzle but also your own state of mind. It's like the light helps you realize, "Oh, I'm not just struggling with this piece. I'm also feeling anxious because I can't find where it fits."

This tool is a moment of clarity. When someone throws a hurtful comment your way, instead of immediately getting lost in a swirl of emotions, you switch on your "Emotional Flashlight." You pause and analyze—Why did that comment sting? Is it tapping into an insecurity or a past experience? Understanding the 'why' helps you figure out the 'how'—how to cope, how to respond, or how to let it go.

The best part? The more you use this tool, the better you get at using it. You start to notice patterns—like, "Hey, I always get upset when someone questions my identity." Understanding these triggers is like becoming an expert at a certain section of your puzzle. You know it. Well, you can complete it even in low light.

Plus, the "Emotional Flashlight" isn't just for you. When you use it, you show others how to shine a light on their own feelings, too. Maybe they'll pick one up themselves and start getting better at handling their emotions. It's like handing out mini flashlights to everyone in the room, making the whole space brighter and everyone's puzzles a little easier to complete.

Next Up Is The "Support Network Map

The "Support Network Map" is super useful. Think of it as a blueprint that shows you where your helpers are stationed around your puzzle. Each person on the map has their own unique skills—some are great at finding those edge pieces, while others excel at filling in those tricky middle sections. Some might be there for emotional support, offering a pep talk when you feel like you'll never finish your puzzle. Others might be logistical supporters, like folks who know how to navigate healthcare systems or handle legal questions you might have.

This isn't just a "who's who" of friendly faces. It's a practical guide. If you're feeling the emotional strain, you can look at your map and think, "Ah, Aunt Sara is great with emotional stuff. I'll give her a call." Or if you're facing discrimination at work or school, you can pinpoint that friend or mentor who knows the rules and can give you solid advice. It's like knowing exactly which puzzle buddy excels at sky sections and calling them over when you're stuck on a cloud piece.

Even cooler? Your "Support Network Map" is a living document. As you grow, meet new people, and your needs change, you can update it. Maybe you meet someone who's an ace at tricky 3D puzzles, and they become your go-to for complex problems.

But remember, a map is a two-way street. While it helps you know who to reach out to, it also reminds you to check in with these folks, see how they're doing, and offer your own skills in return. It's like a puzzle co-op. Everyone's working on their own masterpiece, but you're all sharing tips and tricks.

And hey, the power of the "Support Network Map" can stretch even further. You can introduce people within your network to each other. It's like saying, "Hey, you're both great at ocean scenes. You should team up." This way, the support network grows stronger and more interconnected, making everyone's puzzle journey a bit smoother.

Fact Sheet

The "Fact Sheet" is a pretty handy tool, almost like the cheat sheet you'd keep beside you for the hardest parts of your puzzle. It's filled with quick, digestible facts and counter-arguments to common misconceptions about being LGBTQIA+. When someone throws a curveball like, "Isn't this just a lifestyle choice?" or "You're too young to know your gender," you can easily refer to your "Fact Sheet" and provide an informed response. It's like having a guidebook that tells you the optimal way to tackle a complicated sky full of similar-looking cloud pieces.

But it's not just about having many canned responses. The "Fact Sheet" should be tailored to you, focusing on areas where you often face questions or prejudice. If you're often confronted about your identity, you could have statistics or studies that support you. Suppose people often make incorrect assumptions about your relationships. In that case, you can include key points that clarify what your relationships are actually like. It's like having a section in your puzzle guide that specifically deals with those oddly shaped pieces everyone keeps tripping over.

The beauty of the "Fact Sheet" is its flexibility. You can adjust it as you learn more and as societal attitudes change. If you read a new study or article that offers a better way to explain something, update the sheet! And, just like you would with a tough puzzle, don't hesitate to consult experts or trustworthy sources to make your "Fact Sheet" as strong as possible.

Another thing

The "Fact Sheet" is also for you, not just for educating others. On days when you're feeling down or questioning yourself because of the constant noise around you, looking at your "Fact Sheet" can be affirming. It reminds you that, yes, you are valid, and no, you don't have to accept misinformation. It's like reading the puzzle rules when you're stuck to remind yourself that you're on the right track.

Boundary Fence

The "Boundary Fence" is crucial because it's your personal safeguard, kind of like a do-not-cross line that you put around your puzzle area. Imagine you're deeply focused on fitting those intricate pieces together, and someone keeps reaching over, meddling with pieces, or making unsolicited comments. That's where your "Boundary Fence" comes into play. It's your way of saying, "This is my space. Respect it."

Setting up this "fence" is more than just a one-time action. It's an ongoing process. You have to decide what's acceptable to you and what's not. Maybe you're okay with people asking general questions about your identity but not cool with prying into your personal life. Or perhaps you don't mind jokes, but only if they're not at the expense of your identity. It's like deciding what rules you have for people who want to join you in working on your puzzle. Can they add pieces? Can they comment? Or are they just there to admire and support?

Once you've decided what your boundaries are, the next step is communication. You have to let people know what lines shouldn't be crossed. It could be as straightforward as saying, "I don't like it when you say that," or as subtle as steering a conversation away from topics you're not comfortable discussing. It's like putting up a little sign next to your puzzle that lays out the rules for anyone approaching it.

Enforcing these boundaries is crucial. If someone keeps ignoring your "Boundary Fence," you might need to take further steps. That could be anything from a more serious conversation to limiting contact with that person. It's like having a backup plan in case someone keeps messing with your puzzle despite your clear rules. Maybe you move your table to a different room, or perhaps you decide that some people aren't allowed in your puzzle-building space at all.

In the long run, having a well-maintained "Boundary Fence" makes your life a lot easier. It helps keep your emotional space safe, letting you focus on building your puzzle—the intricate, beautiful picture that represents you—without unnecessary distractions or stress.

Self-Care Package

When you're working on a tricky puzzle, sometimes the pieces just don't fit right away. It's frustrating, right? You might feel like giving up. Well, life can be like that puzzle sometimes. Things don't always go your way. You make mistakes. People might not understand you. You're trying to find out who you are, and that's not easy.

That's where the "Self-Care Package" comes in. Imagine it like a special toolbox you've got right next to you while working on that hard puzzle. You know, the puzzle that's kinda like your life. This toolbox doesn't have hammers or screwdrivers. It's packed with stuff that just makes you feel good.

What's in this Self-Care Package? Maybe it's a playlist of your favorite songs, the ones that get your spirits up or make you feel like dancing. Music is like that corner piece in a puzzle. It helps frame everything else you're feeling.

What else? A comforting snack can also be a game-changer. Sometimes, a little bit of chocolate or a handful of your favorite chips can give you that extra push. It's like finding a puzzle piece you've been searching for. It brings a smile to your face and helps you keep going.

Don't forget a cozy blanket. When things get tough, wrapping yourself up can feel like putting the edge pieces of the puzzle together—it gives you a sense of boundary and safety.

But hey, a Self-Care Package isn't just stuff. It can include actions, too. Maybe you take a five-minute break to doodle when you're stressed. Or you call a friend who's really good at making you laugh. These actions are like those puzzle strategies you develop to get through the hard sections. You find out what works for you, and you stick with it.

Remember, life's like a big, complex puzzle. And just like any puzzler, you'll need some help along the way. Your Self-Care Package isn't cheating. It's your personal set of tools to help you keep going. Because sometimes, you need a little comfort to put the pieces together.

Change Agent Badge, you've got your Self-Care Package, your trusty toolbox to get you through the puzzle of life. But what about when you look up and see others struggling with their own puzzles? You realize some people don't even have all the pieces they need. That's messed up, right? That's where your "Change Agent Badge" comes in.

Think of the Change Agent Badge as this super special puzzle piece that doesn't just fit into your own puzzle but can connect with other people's puzzles, too. This piece has the power to help not just you but everyone around you. Cool, huh?

What's in the Change Agent Badge? a list of social issues that matter to you. Maybe it's LGBTQIA+ rights, fighting against bullying, or making sure everyone gets an equal shot at a good education. Knowing what you care about is like having a picture of the puzzle on the box—it gives you an idea of what you're working toward.

You'll want to have links to petitions. These are your tools for change, kind of like those flat-edged pieces that help you build the frame of the puzzle. Signing a petition is one way to say, "Hey, this matters!" and to get other people to notice it, too.

But why stop there? You can also include contact info for your local representatives. Yeah, it might seem a bit grown-up, but remember, you're figuring out what growing up means. Reaching out to them is like connecting a really tricky piece of the puzzle. It might take some time and effort, but once it's in, it can change the whole picture.

Why is the Change Agent Badge important? Well, it's like this. Imagine everyone's working on their own puzzles, but some people are missing pieces because they've been handed an incomplete set. That's not fair, and it makes their puzzle way harder to solve. Your Change Agent Badge is your way of helping them get those missing pieces.

Remember, you're not just working on your own puzzle in life. you're part of a bigger picture where everyone's puzzles connect. And when you help others, you're not just being kind. you're making the whole picture better. That's what wearing your Change Agent Badge is all about.

Pause Button.

Yep, that's right—a moment to step back and breathe when someone throws a curveball your way. Take a second to collect yourself before responding. It's like taking a step back from your puzzle to see where the next piece fits best.

The "Pause Button" is a super useful tool you want to have front and center in your toolkit. Imagine you're deep into fitting puzzle pieces, and someone just blurts out something that rattles you. Maybe they say your puzzle is "wrong" or "doesn't make sense." Instead of reacting right away, which might mess up your puzzle even more, you hit that "Pause Button."

Please think of this pause as stepping back from your puzzle and looking at it from a distance. When you're too close, it's hard to see where everything fits. Taking a moment to breathe helps you get a better view of the whole picture. You're giving yourself the time to think, "Is this a situation I want to address now? Do I need more time to think it over? What's the best way to handle this?"

And here's the cool part

hitting the "Pause Button" doesn't just help you. It can also affect the people around you. When they see you taking a step back, it's like a signal that says, "Hey, let's all think before we speak." Sometimes, that's all it takes to change the vibe of a situation. It shows you're thoughtful and careful, both about your own puzzle and the puzzles of those around you.

The "Pause Button" is a tool that helps you in multiple ways. It not only gives you the space to react in the way you think is best, but it also sets a tone of respect and thoughtfulness. Next time things get tricky, whether with your puzzle or with people, don't forget to hit that "Pause Button" and give yourself the space you need.

Puzzle Protectors

Ah, the "Puzzle Protectors"—they're the gems in your toolkit. Imagine you're at a big puzzle-building party. Some folks are hovering around, saying your puzzle doesn't look right or should be more like theirs. That's when your "Puzzle Protectors" step in, forming a circle around you and your masterpiece. They're not just standing there. they're actively helping you fit your pieces together, occasionally glancing up to shoot a "mind your own business" look at the naysayers.

The cool thing about "Puzzle Protectors" is they come in all shapes and sizes. They could be your family, your friends, or mentors. They might be people from online communities or folks you meet at support groups. These are the people who get it, who understand that every puzzle is unique and beautiful in its own way.

When you're navigating tricky situations, these protectors can offer more than emotional support. They can offer real, practical advice. Maybe they've faced similar challenges and can tell you how they handled it. Perhaps they can share resources, like books websites, or even introduce you to others who can help. They're your go-to people when you're lost or stuck and don't know where the next piece fits.

In times of trouble, your "Puzzle Protectors" are your safety net. They remind you that, despite the challenges, you're not alone. Your puzzle might be yours alone to complete, but that doesn't mean you have to do it without support. Keep those "Puzzle Protectors" close. They make the whole process a lot more doable and a lot less lonely.

Education Cards

"Education Cards" are clutch. Think of them as your go-to quick guides, kinda like cheat sheets for your puzzle journey. Let's say you're deep in concentration, fitting a piece into your puzzle, and someone walks up and says, "Why can't you just be normal?" Instead of getting tangled in a long debate or feeling upset, you can whip out an "Education Card."

An "Education Card" could be a clear, simple statement that explains a concept they might not understand. For instance, you might say, "What's normal for you might not be for me. Gender is complex." The idea here is not to get into a full-blown conversation but to give them a nugget of info that makes them think. It's kinda like when a puzzle piece is turned the wrong way. A quick flip puts it right back where it belongs.

These cards are also super helpful because they're not just for others. They're for you, too. They help you articulate your thoughts and feelings, giving you confidence in situations that can otherwise be kinda nerve-wracking. Plus, having these ready means you're not caught off guard. You're prepared to tackle misunderstandings head-on.

And hey, if you're really lucky, your "Education Card" might just be the spark that gets someone else curious about learning more. Maybe they'll even start working on their own puzzle with a newfound appreciation for all the different kinds there can be. Having a few "Education Cards" up your sleeve? Definitely a smart move.

Boundary Markers

"Boundary Markers" are essential. Think of them as the edges of your puzzle table. They outline the space you're working in and keep your pieces from falling off and getting lost. But "Boundary Markers" aren't just physical. They're emotional and mental, too.

Let's say someone keeps tossing their own puzzle pieces onto your table, confusing your work. A "Boundary Marker" could be a clear, firm statement like, "Hey, this is my puzzle, and these are my pieces. Please respect that." It's your way of saying, "This is my space, and it's not up for grabs."

And hey, boundaries aren't just about keeping things out. They're also about knowing when to let things in. Like, maybe you've got a friend who's super supportive but a little too eager to help with your puzzle. A "Boundary Marker" here might be saying, "I appreciate your help, but I need to figure out some of these pieces on my own."

Sometimes, you might have to relocate your puzzle altogether, away from people who just can't respect your boundaries. That could mean anything from limiting your time with certain family members to choosing a different social setting where you feel more accepted. It's all about creating a safe and comfortable space where your puzzle—aka you—can thrive.

"Boundary Markers" are a big deal. They're like your puzzle's security guards, keeping the space safe and letting you focus on creating something amazing. And remember, setting boundaries isn't being mean. It's a form of self-care. After all, you can't complete your puzzle if you're constantly worrying about someone messing it up.

"Self-Care Kit"

a "Self-Care Kit" is a must-have. Think of it as the comfy chair you sit in while working on your puzzle or the favorite snack you keep nearby. It's all about creating an environment where you can relax and recharge when things get tough.

What goes into this kit? Well, it's different for everyone. For some, it might be a playlist of uplifting or calming tunes that can reset your mood. You hit play, and it's like stepping back to look at the sections of your puzzle that you've already nailed. The music reminds you that you've got this, even when some pieces are still missing or confusing.

Journals are another great tool. Writing down your thoughts and feelings can help make sense of them. It's like taking a snapshot of your puzzle at different stages—you can look back and see how far you've come and what challenges you've already conquered.

Emergency hotlines or supportive apps can be life-savers, like a puzzle guide for when you're totally stuck and don't know what to do next. These resources offer professional advice and emotional support when you need it most.

And don't underestimate the power of simple things like a warm bath, a favorite book, or even a quick walk outside. These are like little puzzle breaks, moments where you step away and come back refreshed, with new energy to tackle the tricky parts.

The "Self-Care Kit" isn't just for emergencies, though. It's good to dip into it regularly to keep yourself balanced and ready for whatever comes your way. It's like dusting off your puzzle table or straightening out the pieces now and then—you're keeping your workspace and your headspace clean and organized.

Your "Self-Care Kit" is more than just a comfort zone. It's a vital part of the process, making sure you've got the energy and focus to keep building your puzzle, no matter what challenges you face.

Activism Toolkit

You bet the "Activism Toolkit" is like the bonus pack of special pieces you bring out when it's time to make your puzzle even more awesome. But this toolkit isn't just for you—it's for the whole room of puzzle builders. It helps level the playing field so everyone has a fair shot at completing their masterpieces.

A list of local and national organizations is key. Supporting groups that fight for LGBTQIA+ rights is like pooling together resources to buy a massive, deluxe set of puzzle pieces that everyone in the room can use. Whether it's through donating, volunteering, or spreading the word, backing these organizations helps push for change on a larger scale.

How-to guides on talking to policymakers can be invaluable. Think of it like a puzzle strategy guidebook. It gives you tips and tactics on how to approach those who hold the power to enact meaningful change. Maybe it's tips on what to say during a meeting, how to write an impactful letter or even steps on how to start a petition. With this guide, you're not just placing your own pieces—you're influencing how the whole game is played.

Social media templates are also a good addition. Quick posts you can share that inform and inspire others are like handing out mini-tutorials to everyone in the puzzle room. They offer a simple way for anyone to contribute to the bigger cause, even if it's just by clicking the "share" button.

Then, you might want to add some recommended reading or documentaries. These are the deeper dives, the inside looks at the challenges and triumphs in the LGBTQIA+ community. It's like studying the work of puzzle masters, learning new techniques, and gaining insights that you can bring back to your own project and to others in the room.

And remember, activism isn't a one-size-fits-all kind of deal. Some people might be up for leading a protest, while others are more comfortable working behind the scenes. The important thing is that everyone is contributing in their own way, just like how each person's puzzle is unique but equally valuable.

Your "Activism Toolkit" isn't just another box of puzzle pieces. It's the game-changer, the thing that helps not just you but everyone in the room creates puzzles that are richer, more diverse, and way more meaningful.

By gathering these tools and strategies, you're preparing yourself to face prejudice head-on and bounce back stronger. Each time you use one, you're not just protecting your puzzle. You're also making it easier for everyone else in the room to focus on theirs. And that's resilience—being able to keep building your masterpiece, no matter what gets thrown your way.

Importance Of Support Networks And Allies

you're piecing together your life puzzle, right? And sometimes, those pieces just won't fit, no matter how hard you try. It's like you're doing this big, complicated jigsaw puzzle, but you're missing the box that shows what the finished picture is supposed to look like. Kinda tough, huh? That's where support networks and allies come into play.

Puzzle Buddies

You've got a ton of puzzle pieces scattered on the table in front of you. Some pieces look similar, some are confusing, and some are just plain elusive. It's the same with life's challenges. they're all over the place. Sometimes, no matter how hard you look, you can't find that one piece that fits perfectly.

Enter your puzzle buddies. These could be your friends, your family, teachers, or even mentors. They slide up to the table, take a seat, and start helping you sort through the mess. They don't grab the pieces and jam them into your puzzle for you—that's your job. But they might help you turn the pieces around so you can see them from a different angle.

For example, say you're struggling with your identity and how to fit into a world that doesn't always get you. A good puzzle buddy could be that friend who listens without judgment, who says, "I hear you," and maybe shares their own story to help you feel less alone. They help you see that even if the pieces of your puzzle are complex, they're still yours, and that's what makes them valuable.

Or maybe you're feeling super stressed because you're dealing with tough stuff like school pressure, family expectations, or societal norms about who you should be. A puzzle buddy in your support network might be a parent or a teacher who helps you see the bigger picture. They remind you that it's okay not to have all the answers right now, and they offer strategies that have worked for them or others. They're like the person who shows you that sometimes it helps to work on a small section of the puzzle to give you the confidence to tackle the rest.

But puzzle buddies aren't just there for the hard times. They also celebrate your wins with you, big or small. Manage to fit a few more pieces into your puzzle? They're the ones giving you a high-five or a hug, cheering you on, and reminding you how awesome you are. This is super important because, let's face it, putting together a puzzle can be long and sometimes tedious work. Those mini-celebrations help keep your spirits up and your eyes on the prize.

When you're sifting through the pieces of your life, trying to figure out where each one fits, remember you don't have to do it alone. Your puzzle buddies are there, helping you sort the edge pieces from the middle pieces, offering a fresh perspective, and reminding you that every piece has its place, even if it takes a while to find it. With them by your side, that tricky, beautiful puzzle of yours will start to come together, piece by piece.

A Support Network

let's talk more about that support network. These are the folks who really get you and man, they can make a world of difference when you're knee-deep in puzzle pieces that just don't seem to fit anywhere.

Family

Now, not everyone's family is super supportive, but if yours is, that's like striking gold in the puzzle world. They've known you for a long time, maybe even since you were a tiny puzzle with just a few pieces. They can be the ones who remind you of your strengths when you're feeling lost. In the puzzle analogy, think of them as the ones who help you find the corner pieces—the fundamentals that anchor everything else. With those in place, the rest starts to become a bit clearer and a bit easier to manage.

Friends

Then you've got friends, the buddies you choose for yourself. These folks might not know you as long as your family has, but they understand the you that you are right now. They're the ones who'll sit with you for hours, maybe munching on snacks, as you both try to find the right pieces that fit. Suppose your family helps with the corner pieces. In that case, your friends are like the teammates who help you sort the colors or patterns, breaking down a huge task into smaller, more manageable sections.

Teachers And Mentors

But hey, let's not forget about teachers and mentors. These are the people who've been around the block a few times. They've seen a lot of puzzles in their day and have picked up a trick or two that they can share. Say you're stuck on a specific area, like figuring out what you want to do in the future or how to be more confident in yourself. A teacher or mentor can offer you some solid advice, almost like showing you a strategy for tackling the sky in a jigsaw puzzle when all the pieces look almost the same. They give you a new approach, a fresh way of seeing things, that can help you move forward when you're stuck.

What's super cool about a support network is that it can be a mix of all these people—family, friends, teachers, mentors. Each brings something different to the table. When you're stuck or frustrated, they offer a fresh pair of eyes to look at the mess of pieces before you. And when you finally find where a stubborn piece goes, they're the first to cheer you on.

Remember, puzzles are tricky. Sometimes, you'll be super into it, finding piece after piece, and it feels like you're on a roll. Other times, it's like every piece you pick up just doesn't fit. Your support network is there for all of it, through the ups and the downs. With their help, the full picture of who you are and who you're becoming gets a little clearer each day. And that's pretty awesome.

Allies

Allies listen. Even if they don't get everything you're going through, they're willing to lend an ear. Say you're struggling with something that they've never experienced. While they might not be able to offer advice from a "been there, done that" perspective, just the act of listening can be huge. It's kinda like when you're stuck on a part of your puzzle, and someone walks by, takes a quick look, and says, "Have you tried flipping that piece over?" Sometimes, a fresh perspective from outside your usual circle can offer new insights.

They're the defenders of puzzles everywhere. If they see someone messing with your puzzle—like bullying you or treating you unfairly because of who you are—they're not gonna stand by and watch. They'll step up and say something. It's like if someone tried to scatter your puzzle pieces, an ally would be the person who helps you gather them back up or even confronts the puzzle-wrecker. They might not fully understand why each piece is so important to you, but they respect your right to piece together your puzzle in peace.

Allies are learners. Maybe their own puzzles are pretty straightforward or look different from yours. Maybe they've never had to question their pieces or how they fit. But they're willing to learn from your experience to better understand the complexities that come with piecing together a puzzle like yours. This is super helpful because the more they understand, the better allies they can be. It's a win-win situation for everyone involved.

What's cool about allies is that they can come from anywhere. They could be classmates, co-workers, or even people from online communities. You might find allies in places you never expected, like a club at school or during a community event. Wherever they come from, they bring something valuable to your life.

The gift of solidarity, of standing up for you when you most need it, and sometimes even of standing up for others whose puzzles are still a jumbled mess on the table.

While they may not get your puzzle in the same way your core support network does, allies play an important role in your life. They might not be the ones sitting down with you for hours sorting through every single piece, but they're the ones guarding the table, making sure you have the space and respect you need to work on your puzzle your way. And that's pretty awesome.

Why are these puzzle buddies so important? Well, imagine trying to complete a puzzle with pieces missing or, even worse, people actively hiding your pieces. Not cool, right? Your support network and allies help make sure that doesn't happen. They can help you find missing pieces or defend your puzzle from folks who just don't get how important it is.

You're deep in puzzle-solving mode, right? You're squinting at pieces, holding them up to the light, trying to figure out where they fit. Now imagine someone comes along and either hides a piece or, even worse, takes one away. That's a real buzzkill. You're left with a puzzle that can't be completed, and that can make you feel incomplete, too.

Now, that's where your support network comes into play. These are the people who make sure all your pieces are on the table, visible, and ready for you to place where they belong. If a piece goes missing—like, say, you're feeling down, or you're dealing with something really tough—they help you find it. It's like they come equipped with a puzzle piece detector, helping you locate that crucial piece that brings the whole picture into focus.

Your support network knows you, they understand your struggles, and they're invested in helping you succeed. If a piece goes missing because you're grappling with self-doubt, they remind you of your worth and help you find your self-confidence again. Suppose you're facing external challenges like prejudice or ignorance. In that case, they're the ones who help you navigate these obstacles like a guide helping you find the hidden path through a maze of pieces.

Embracing Your Authentic Self

Embracing and celebrating your gender identity is like finding that last corner piece of your puzzle and snapping it into place. It just feels right, you know? Once you've got those corners and edges sorted, it becomes a whole lot easier to fill in the middle, and you start to see the bigger picture. That's what embracing your identity does—it gives you the framework to understand the rest of yourself better.

Discovering Your Unique Piece

In the intricate puzzle of gender identity, each individual holds a unique piece that contributes to the beautiful mosaic of human diversity. Embracing and celebrating one's gender identity is a journey of self-discovery and self-acceptance, filled with moments of reflection, growth, and empowerment. Whether you identify as male, female, non-binary, or anywhere along the gender spectrum, your identity is valid and worthy of celebration.

Breaking Free From Societal Expectations

Society often imposes rigid norms and expectations around gender, dictating how individuals should look, behave, and express themselves. Breaking free from these constraints requires courage and authenticity, as well as a willingness to challenge societal norms and embrace your true self. Embracing your gender identity means rejecting the limitations imposed by others and living authentically without apology or compromise.

Honoring Your Truth

Your gender identity is an intrinsic part of who you are, deserving of honor and respect. Whether you are cisgender, transgender, or non-binary, your truth is valid and worthy of affirmation. Embracing your gender identity means honoring your innermost feelings and experiences without judgment or self-doubt. By embracing your truth, you pave the way for others to do the same, creating a ripple effect of acceptance and empowerment.

Celebrating Diversity

Gender identity is as diverse and multifaceted as the colors of the rainbow, encompassing a rich tapestry of experiences and expressions. Celebrating diversity means embracing the unique journeys of individuals across the gender spectrum recognizing that there is no one-size-fits-all definition of gender. Whether you express your gender through clothing, pronouns, or personal interests, your identity is valid and worthy of celebration.

Creating Inclusive Spaces

As we celebrate our own gender identities, we must also work to create inclusive spaces where everyone feels seen, heard, and valued. This means challenging gender stereotypes, advocating for gender-affirming policies, and fostering a culture of respect and acceptance. By creating inclusive spaces, we ensure that everyone has the opportunity to embrace and celebrate their gender identity without fear of discrimination or prejudice.

Empowering Others

As you embrace and celebrate your own gender identity, remember to lift others up and empower them to do the same. Whether through mentorship, activism, or simply leading by example, you have the power to make a difference in the lives of others. By standing proudly in your truth, you inspire others to do the same, creating a ripple effect of empowerment and liberation across communities and generations.

In the grand puzzle of life, embracing and celebrating your gender identity is a transformative act of self-love and empowerment. By honoring your truth, breaking free from societal expectations, and creating inclusive spaces for all, you contribute to a world where everyone can live authentically and without fear. Together, let us celebrate the rich diversity of gender identity and create a future where all individuals are free to be their true selves, unapologetically and without reservation.

And here's the cool part - puzzles are meant to be seen. So go ahead and show off your completed sections. Celebrate your identity with people who matter, whether that's marching in a parade, joining an LGBTQIA+ group, or just living openly as yourself. Remember, the more authentic you are, the easier it becomes for others to find and place their own puzzle pieces, too.

Tips For Building Self-Confidence And Self-Acceptance

Building self-confidence and self-acceptance is like working on different sections of your puzzle at the same time. You might be doing great at fitting together the sky pieces, but those tricky water sections? They take a bit more effort. It's a balance, and both parts are crucial for seeing the whole picture of who you are.

Small Wins

When you're building a puzzle, you don't just dump out all the pieces and expect it to come together instantly, right? Nah, you start small—maybe finding all the edge pieces or sorting by color. Each little win sets you up for the making the overall puzzle less daunting. That's the magic of "small wins" in boosting your self-confidence.

Setting Small Goals

You gotta know what your "small goals" are. For some, speaking up in class can be a big deal, especially if you're usually quiet or nervous. For others, maybe it's finally joining that club you've always been interested in or trying your hand at painting even though you think you're bad at art.

The trick is to choose goals that are a tiny bit outside your comfort zone but not so far out that they seem impossible. For example, if you've never talked in class before, don't aim to lead the whole discussion the first time. Maybe start by challenging yourself to make one comment or ask one question.

The Feeling Of A Win

Every time you reach one of these small goals, you're gonna feel like you've just snapped a puzzle piece into its perfect spot. It's satisfying and gives you this little burst of, "Hey, I did it!" That's your confidence growing, piece by piece.

Momentum Builds Up

Once you've got a few pieces in place, you'll notice something awesome happening—you start to build momentum. Speaking up in class once makes it easier to do it again. Painting one picture makes you more willing to paint another. It's like when you start getting sections of your puzzle together. It becomes easier and faster to find where the next pieces go.

Adjusting Goals

As you keep hitting those small wins, you might find that goals you once thought were big and scary now seem way more doable. That's your cue to adjust your goals and make them a bit bigger. Maybe now you aim to answer two questions in class or paint a more complicated picture.

The Ripple Effect

The coolest part? These small wins don't just boost your confidence in one area. they often create a ripple effect. speaking up in class might make you more confident in social situations. Painting might make you realize you're more creative than you thought, giving you the confidence to try other new things. It's like how completing one section of the puzzle makes the next sections seem less intimidating.

Remember, the point isn't to rush through and get to a "finished" you. Just like a puzzle, you're a work in progress, and that's totally okay. Every small win is a piece of the larger picture of who you are, so celebrate each one. After all, it's those individual pieces that make the completed puzzle so amazing.

Skill Building

Skill building is like focusing on a specific section of your puzzle. Say you've got a part with lots of blues and greens—it's complicated, and it's gonna take time to get it right. But the more you work at it, the easier it becomes to spot the pieces that fit. The same goes for building a skill. The more you practice, the more pieces of that skill's "puzzle" fit together.

Picking The Skill

First things first - you've got to decide what skill you want to focus on. This is your chance to zero in on a hobby or interest that you've always wanted to get better at. Love drawing? Awesome, there's your skill. Have you ever been curious about how apps get made? Cool, you can start learning to code. The key is picking something that excites you. That way, practice won't feel like a chore.

Getting Started

You've picked your skill. Now what? Time to dive in! But remember, you don't have to be an expert overnight. If you're learning to play the guitar, maybe start by learning a few chords. If you're into cooking, try mastering a simple recipe first. Think of it as finding the edge pieces of this skill "section" of your puzzle—you're setting up the framework.

Consistent Practice

The next step is to keep at it. Just like a puzzle doesn't come together if you only work on it once and then ignore it, skills require consistent practice. Make a schedule or set reminders, whatever helps you keep going. Each practice session is like adding a few more pieces to your puzzle.

Tracking Progress

Here's a super satisfying part

seeing yourself get better. Maybe you notice that you can play a song on the guitar without stumbling, or you cook a meal that actually tastes good. Every time you see progress, it's a boost to your confidence. It's like finally getting all the difficult blue and green pieces to fit together. You can look at it and say, "Wow, I did that."

Leveling Up

As you get better at this skill, you'll find that what used to be hard becomes easy. That's your cue to take it to the next level. If you were learning to code, maybe move on to a more complex project. If it was sports, try more advanced techniques. It's like you've finished a section of the puzzle, and now you're ready to tackle the next one, armed with all the experience you've gained.

The Confidence Boost

When you build a skill, it's not just about getting better at that specific thing. It's also a big boost to your self-confidence. Each time you master a level of your chosen skill, it's a reminder that you can set goals and achieve them. And that sort of confidence? It spills over into other parts of your life, helping you snap more pieces into your overall puzzle of self-confidence and self-acceptance.

Go ahead, pick a skill, and start fitting those puzzle pieces together. You'll be amazed at how good it feels to see that section come to life.

Positive Affirmations

Positive affirmations are like the picture on the front of the puzzle box. You know, the image that shows you what you're working toward. Sometimes, when you're neck-deep in sorting through puzzle pieces—especially the confusing ones—it's easy to lose sight of the bigger picture. That's when you can glance at the box to remind yourself, "Oh yeah, this is gonna look awesome when it's done." Positive affirmations serve the same purpose for your self-confidence and self-acceptance journey.

Crafting Your Affirmations

You gotta decide what your positive affirmations are. These are statements that resonate with you and make you feel good about who you are. They can be simple stuff like, "I'm a good friend" or "I'm strong." The point is they should be true and meaningful to you. It's like picking a puzzle that you're excited to complete, not just any random one off the shelf.

Write 'Em Down

Take some time to write these affirmations down. You could jot them in a notebook, type them on your phone, or even write them on sticky notes to put around your room. Make it something you can easily access. It's like keeping the puzzle box nearby when you're working on the puzzle. you want to be able to easily see it for reference.

When To Use Them

There will be times when you're feeling down or doubting yourself. Maybe you messed up on something, or you're just having a blah day. That's when you pull out your affirmations. Read them aloud or in your head, but really focus on the words. This is your puzzle box moment. It's a way to remind yourself that the end picture is made up of many pieces, and just because one piece is missing or misplaced, it doesn't ruin the whole thing.

Make It A Habit

The more you use your positive affirmations, the more natural it'll feel. Over time, you'll start to internalize these affirmations as part of your self-talk. It's like the more you work on puzzles, the better you get at spotting where pieces should go, even without constantly checking the box.

The Boost

Here's the cool part - these affirmations can actually help improve your mood and boost your self-confidence in the moment. Just like glancing at the completed picture on a puzzle box can give you a burst of motivation, your affirmations can give you a quick shot of self-assurance.

Update And Tweak

Feel free to update or tweak your affirmations as you go along. As you grow and change, your "puzzle" evolves, too. New pieces come in, and some might not fit like they used to. And that's perfectly okay. Update your affirmations to match the person you're becoming.

Next time you're feeling stuck or unsure, just remember to check your "puzzle box"—your positive affirmations. They'll remind you of the awesome picture you're working towards, one piece at a time.

Now, onto self-acceptance. This is the harder part of the puzzle, with all those weird-shaped pieces that don't seem to fit anywhere until you really look.

Self-Reflection

Self-reflection is like taking a moment to step back and look at your puzzle in progress. Sometimes, when you're too close to the puzzle, you might miss where certain pieces should go. You get stuck in the details and forget to see the bigger picture. But when you step back, you can see the gaps and the pieces that need to be moved. Self-reflection works the same way—it helps you understand the bigger picture of yourself, including your thoughts and feelings.

Finding Your Space

The first step in self-reflection is finding a good spot where you can think without distractions. Maybe it's your room, a quiet spot in a park, or even just a corner of your home where you feel comfy. It would help if you had a "puzzle table" where you could spread out your pieces—your thoughts and feelings—without disturbance.

The Process

You can use different methods for self-reflection. Some folks like to meditate, focusing on their breath to clear their minds. Others prefer writing in a journal, jotting down thoughts, feelings, or even doodles that help them make sense of things. Choose a method that feels right for you. It's like choosing whether to sort your puzzle pieces by color, edge or some other method—there's no one right way to do it.

Asking The Right Questions

When you're reflecting, consider asking yourself some questions. Things like, "Why did that comment bother me?" or "Why did I feel so happy when that happened?" These questions help you dig deeper into your thoughts and feelings. It's like examining each puzzle piece carefully to figure out where it might fit.

Understanding Feelings

The goal isn't to judge yourself but to understand why you feel the way you do. Maybe you realize you felt upset because you were already having a tough day, or maybe you find out that certain things trigger happiness or sadness. Understanding the "why" is like finding a piece you've been searching for—it helps complete the picture.

Acceptance

The final step is acceptance. This doesn't mean you have to like every thought or feeling you have, but understanding them helps you accept that they're a part of you, for better or worse. Each thought or emotion is a piece of your puzzle, and even if it's a weirdly shaped one or has colors you don't like, it still has a place.

The Ongoing Puzzle

Remember, self-reflection isn't a one-time deal. Your puzzle is always changing, with new pieces showing up and others changing shape. Regular moments of reflection help you keep up with these changes so that your puzzle—your understanding of yourself—stays current.

make some time for self-reflection. It's your chance to step back, look at your puzzle, and get a clearer picture of yourself. And the clearer that picture gets, the easier it is to find where the next pieces go.

Talk It Out

Talking it out with someone is like inviting a friend over to help you with a tricky puzzle. You've been staring at this thing for hours, trying to jam pieces together that just don't seem to fit. Then your buddy comes along, takes one look, and goes, "Hey, that piece goes over there!" And suddenly, it's like a lightbulb goes on. Sometimes, a fresh perspective can make all the difference in helping you see where your "pieces"—whether they're thoughts, feelings, or challenges—really belong.

Choosing Your Puzzle Partner

you need to pick who you're going to talk to. Not everyone is good at puzzles, and not everyone is good at giving advice or emotional support. Your go-to could be a trusted friend, a family member, or even a counselor or therapist.

Whoever it is, it should be someone who makes you feel heard and understood. Think of it as choosing the best puzzle partner—one who won't just hog all the edge pieces!

Starting The Conversation

Once you've picked your person, it's time to dive in. Share what you're going through, but remember, you don't have to dump out all the puzzle pieces at once. You can start small, sharing just a piece or two of what's on your mind. This gives the other person a chance to absorb what you're saying and offer their perspective. The goal here is to find where these emotional or mental "pieces" fit into your bigger life puzzle.

Listening And Learning

Sometimes, the advice or perspective you get might surprise you. It could be something you never even considered. Be open to this new viewpoint. You know how sometimes you're doing a puzzle, and you're sure a piece fits in one place, but then someone shows you it actually belongs somewhere else? It can be a real "a-ha!" moment. The same goes for talking it out with someone. their insights can suddenly make things click into place.

Sorting Out Your Feelings

Talking things out can help you better understand your feelings, even if the other person doesn't have all the answers. Sometimes, just the act of talking can make things clearer. You're essentially laying out your puzzle pieces, taking a good look at them, and figuring out where they might go. This process alone can be incredibly helpful in sorting out your emotions and thoughts.

Reevaluating And Reorganizing

After you've had a good chat, take some time to reflect on what was said. How does this new perspective fit into your life puzzle? Do you need to move some pieces around? Or did you find the perfect spot for a piece that had been bugging you for ages? This is your chance to reevaluate and reorganize your thoughts and feelings based on the new insights you've gained.

The Lifelong Puzzle

Remember, your life puzzle is never really "done." New pieces keep showing up, and old ones might shift around. That's why it's so helpful to have trusted people you can talk to as your puzzle evolves. They can help you keep the big picture in focus and assist in finding the right spot for new or troubling pieces. Don't be shy about asking for help with your puzzle. Sometimes, another set of eyes is just what you need to see where your pieces belong.

Forgive Yourself

Everyone has pieces in their puzzle that seem out of place. Maybe you said something awkward or didn't do well on a test. It's okay. Those pieces don't define the whole puzzle. They're just a small part of it.

Celebrate The Victories, Even The Small Ones.

Did you find a piece that fits? Awesome! Did you manage to complete a small section? Even better! Each win, no matter how small, is progress, and that's something to be proud of.

Celebrating victories in your life is like relishing those satisfying moments when you find just the right spot for a tricky puzzle piece. The feeling of it clicking into place? Man, that's a good feeling! It doesn't matter if it's just one piece or if you've managed to complete a whole section of your puzzle—each win counts and deserves a little celebration. Because let's be real, puzzles can be hard, and so can life. Taking the time to celebrate makes the challenging parts a lot more manageable.

The Joy Of Small Wins

Do you know how, in a puzzle, sometimes you're stuck for a bit, but then you find one piece that fits, and it feels like a mini victory? Life's like that, too. Maybe you got a better grade than you expected on a quiz, or you finally spoke up in a meeting. These might seem like tiny things, but they're actually pretty big. Why? Because they show you're making progress. Small wins are like the breadcrumbs leading you through the forest—they keep you on the right path.

How To Celebrate

What's the best way to celebrate these moments? Well, it doesn't have to be a big deal. It could be as simple as doing a little happy dance or treating yourself to your favorite snack. Or maybe you take a moment to text a friend who gets it and will cheer you on. The point is to take a moment—any moment—to acknowledge that you did something good. It's like admiring your puzzle every so often instead of just pushing ahead to finish it.

Building Momentum

Each small win helps build your confidence for bigger challenges, both in puzzles and in life. Got a section of the sky done? Now, you're ready to tackle those tricky edge pieces. The same goes for life. Nailed that quiz? You're better prepared for the big test coming up. Each win adds another layer of belief that, yeah, you've got this.

Share The Joy

Don't underestimate the power of sharing your victories with others. When you've placed a particularly tricky piece, it's so much more satisfying to have someone there to high-five you. The shared joy magnifies the feeling of accomplishment. So go ahead and tell your friends or family about your wins. Their cheerleading can make your next challenge seem a whole lot less daunting.

The Never-Ending Puzzle

Remember, your life puzzle will never really be 'complete' in the way a jigsaw puzzle can be finished and framed. You're always adding new pieces—new experiences, challenges, and victories. And that's the fun of it! Life's puzzle is dynamic and ever-changing. So make sure to pause now and then, look at what you've built so far, and celebrate all those pieces that have found their perfect spot.

In short, don't rush through your puzzle so focused on finishing that you forget to enjoy the process. Take time to celebrate each and every piece you successfully place. Each one is a victory, a step forward, and absolutely something to be proud of.

By working on both self-confidence and self-acceptance, you'll see your puzzle come together faster than you think. Sure, it's a complicated puzzle, but it's yours, and every piece you place makes it more and more complete.

Personal Stories Of Empowerment And Authenticity

Personal stories of empowerment and authenticity are like those puzzles you finally complete after a lot of hard work. Each piece, or each experience, adds up to create a clearer picture of who you are. The triumphs feel like those "a-ha" moments when a particularly stubborn piece finally finds its home, and the setbacks, well, they're the misplaced pieces you have to relocate. But each piece matters, and each piece is a part of the bigger picture—your unique, authentic self.

The "Be Yourself" Journey

Imagine a teenager named Alex who always loved music. But in the circle Alex hung out in, sports were a big deal. Alex felt the pressure to fit into that sports-centered world, like trying to force a puzzle piece into a spot where it just doesn't belong. It took a lot of courage for Alex to finally say, "You know what, I'm gonna join the school band." The moment Alex made that decision, it was like finding a whole corner of the puzzle that suddenly fit together perfectly. That decision empowered Alex to be more authentic, to be more, well, Alex.

Coming Out And Finding Community

Or consider Taylor, who identified as non-binary but was nervous about coming out. The fear and secrecy felt like holding onto a puzzle piece that you know has a spot, but you're too afraid to put it down. When Taylor finally opened up to a trusted friend, it was like that piece had found its perfect place. The friend's acceptance and support empowered Taylor to eventually come out to more people, forming a community that became a crucial part of Taylor's support system.

Overcoming Obstacles Through Authenticity

Then there's Jordan, who faced bullying in school. The experience felt like someone had taken some pieces out of Jordan's puzzle, leaving gaps of self-doubt and sadness. It wasn't until Jordan joined an art club and discovered a passion for painting that those missing pieces started to come back. Art became a way for Jordan to express his true feelings and to be authentic. The confidence gained through art made it easier to face and overcome the bullies. It's like Jordan found not just one but several missing puzzle pieces and fit them all into place.

The Power Of Small Actions

These stories show that empowerment and authenticity don't always come from grand or dramatic moments. Sometimes, it's the small choices that make the biggest difference. It could be as simple as choosing to speak your mind in a group setting, standing up for someone else, or even picking up a hobby that you genuinely love. Each small act of authenticity adds another piece to your puzzle, making the overall picture—your life—more complete and more you.

The Whole Picture

The thing about puzzles is the whole picture is made up of individual pieces, and each piece is important. In the same way, each moment or decision in your life that makes you feel empowered and authentic adds up to create the bigger picture of who you are. So celebrate each of those moments because they're all pieces of the fantastic, one-of-a-kind puzzle that is you.

The Ripple Effect Of Alex's Choice

Remember Alex, who loved music but felt trapped in a sports-dominated environment? The decision to join the band didn't just stop at making Alex happy. It created a ripple effect. Seeing Alex embrace this authentic self encouraged others in the social circle to rethink their own choices and passions. It was like Alex placing that corner piece helped others see where their own puzzle pieces might fit. They saw that embracing who you truly are isn't just okay. It's liberating. For Alex, that first step led to bigger things, like performing in concerts and even composing music. Each new milestone added another piece to the growing, complex puzzle.

Taylor's Journey To Advocacy

Taylor didn't stop at finding a supportive community after coming out as non-binary. Empowered by the experience, Taylor became an advocate for LGBTQIA+ awareness in school. The experience was like going from piecing together a small puzzle to tackling something much larger and more complex. Taylor started to understand that authenticity could be empowering not just for oneself but also for others. Sharing personal stories in group discussions, Taylor added pieces to other people's puzzles, helping them to be true to themselves, too.

Jordan Finds A Voice

After discovering a love for art, Jordan decided to use it as a medium to address bullying, creating pieces that encapsulated the emotional struggle and the journey towards self-acceptance. When these pieces were showcased in the school art exhibition, it was like Jordan had put together an entire section of the puzzle for everyone to see. The vulnerability of putting something so personal on public display was scary but also incredibly empowering. It started conversations, changed some attitudes, and, most importantly, it gave Jordan a sense of closure and confidence. It felt like those lost puzzle pieces were not just replaced but upgraded.

The Power Of Ongoing Self-Discovery

The key takeaway here is that the journey to empowerment and authenticity is ongoing. Your puzzle is never really "complete" because you're always growing, learning, and changing. And sometimes, the pieces you find might surprise you—they might not be the shapes or colors you expected. But that's the whole point of the puzzle, isn't it? To surprise you, challenge you, and ultimately, to show you a picture that makes sense.

Whether you're taking that first brave step like Alex, finding your community like Taylor, or discovering a newfound passion like Jordan, remember that each choice you make adds another piece to your unique, evolving puzzle. Celebrate each piece, each moment, because they make up the amazing, complicated, one-of-a-kind masterpiece that is you.

Alex's Broader Impact

Alex's decision to join the school band didn't just transform their own life or encourage immediate friends. It had a broader impact on the school community. Teachers saw this as a teachable moment about individuality, discussing it in classes. Parents' conversations around dinner tables began to shift towards supporting their kids' genuine interests rather than fitting into pre-established norms. Alex became a living example that going against the grain could lead to not only personal happiness but also community growth. It's like Alex's puzzle piece started to form part of other people's puzzles, showing that embracing one's authentic self could lead to widespread positive change.

Taylor's Expanding Community

Empowered by personal growth and a supportive community, Taylor took the advocacy beyond the school premises. By writing blogs and sharing experiences on social media platforms, Taylor connected with people from different backgrounds and countries. It was like taking a single puzzle and realizing it's actually part of a much bigger picture. In this global picture, individual pieces, or stories, fit together to create a broader narrative about acceptance and inclusivity.

Jordan's Art As A Healing Mechanism

Jordan used the art exhibition experience as a stepping stone. It wasn't just about combating bullying. It became about using art as a healing mechanism for personal and collective struggles. Jordan started workshops where kids could paint their feelings, a method to channel their emotions creatively. For Jordan, each painting, each emotion captured, was another piece fitting snugly into their personal puzzle, and each workshop was an opportunity to help others find where their puzzle pieces fit, too.

The Interconnectedness Of Puzzles

What these expanded stories show is that the puzzle of your life isn't isolated. It connects with other people's puzzles, and sometimes, your pieces help to complete someone else's picture. Alex's choice inspired others to follow their passions. Taylor's advocacy became a beacon for those grappling with their gender identity. Jordan's art turned into a form of collective healing.

Long-Term Gains

The empowerment and authenticity these individuals found were not just short-term wins. They were pieces that connected to even bigger pieces, creating a long-term impact. Each of them found a pathway that wasn't just about fitting a piece into their own puzzle but also about adding to the puzzles of a community, a school, or even a generation.

A Continuous Journey

Your puzzle isn't a static image. it's a dynamic, ever-changing tapestry of experiences, decisions, and relationships. It's essential to recognize that while your puzzle will have its gaps and misplaced pieces, it will also have intricate patterns and snugly fitting sections that you should celebrate and appreciate. The puzzle is never truly done, but that's okay because it's not about finishing. it's about the joy and growth that come from placing each piece, one authentic moment at a time.

By acknowledging and celebrating each piece of your puzzle—each step in your journey—you contribute not just to your own sense of self but potentially to a broader, interconnected network of empowerment and authenticity.

Building Your Life Puzzle

A Step-By-Step Guide

1. Know Your Pieces (Identify Goals)

Begin by clarifying your goals and aspirations. Write down what you want to achieve, whether it's coming out to your family, excelling in academics, or pursuing a career in your dream field. By identifying your pieces, you gain clarity on the direction you want your life puzzle to take.

2. Sort Your Edges (Prioritize)

Prioritize your goals by determining which ones are most urgent and important to you. Just as the edge pieces frame the puzzle, these goals provide structure and direction to your journey. Consider factors such as timelines, feasibility, and personal values to guide your prioritization process.

3. Find Pairs (Action Steps)

Break down each goal into actionable steps or tasks. These smaller steps serve as pairs of puzzle pieces that fit together seamlessly, guiding you toward the completion of your larger goals. Be specific and realistic in identifying the actions needed to move closer to your objectives.

4. Connect Sections (Commit To Actions)

Commit to taking action on each of the identified steps. Every action you take is akin to snapping another piece into the puzzle, gradually building momentum and progress toward your goals. Stay disciplined and consistent in following through with your commitments.

5. Keep The Picture In Mind (Track Progress)

Maintain a clear vision of the big picture while tracking your progress. Reflect on how each small step contributes to the realization of your larger goals.

Tracking your progress allows you to stay focused and motivated, even when faced with challenges or setbacks along the way.

6. Don't Force It (Be Realistic)

Be mindful of when to reassess and readjust your approach. If a particular action or strategy isn't yielding the desired results, don't force it. Instead, be open to adapting your approach and exploring alternative solutions that align better with your goals and circumstances.

7. Embrace The Gaps (Learn And Adapt)

Acknowledge that not every piece will fit perfectly right away, and that's okay. Embrace the gaps and view them as opportunities for learning and growth. When you encounter obstacles or setbacks, reflect on the lessons they offer and adapt your strategies accordingly. Remember the LARK Code—Love yourself, Accept yourself, Respect yourself, Know yourself—as a guiding principle in navigating challenges.

8. Celebrate The Connections (Acknowledge Achievements)

Celebrate each milestone and achievement along the way. Every piece you successfully fit into place is a testament to your progress and perseverance. Acknowledge your achievements, no matter how small, and take pride in the progress you've made towards your goals.

9. Keep Going (Maintain Momentum)

Maintain momentum by staying committed to your journey, even when faced with difficulties or uncertainties. Puzzles may be complex and challenging, but the satisfaction of completing them is unparalleled. Keep going, one piece at a time, and trust in your ability to overcome obstacles and achieve your aspirations.

10. Share The Joy (Support And Community)

Remember that you don't have to navigate your life puzzle alone. Share your struggles and triumphs with trusted friends, family members, or mentors who can offer support and guidance. Lean on your community for encouragement and motivation, and be open to providing support to others as they work towards their own goals. Together, you can find strength in each other and collaboratively fit the pieces of your life puzzles into place.

Your life is a puzzle waiting to be assembled, with each goal and aspiration representing a piece waiting to be fit into place. By following these steps and embracing the journey, you can navigate the complexities of life with purpose, resilience, and joy. roll up your sleeves, dive into your puzzle, and remember—you've got this!

Preventing Growth

Understanding Growth Prevention

In the intricate fabric of society, growth prevention refers to the various obstacles and challenges that hinder personal, emotional, and societal development. These barriers can take many forms, including discrimination, inequality, lack of access to resources, and systemic oppression. Understanding the mechanisms of growth prevention is crucial in addressing these barriers and fostering environments where individuals can thrive.

Economic Inequality

One of the most pervasive forms of growth prevention is economic inequality, which creates disparities in access to education, healthcare, and economic opportunities. Limited access to resources can perpetuate cycles of poverty and prevent individuals from reaching their full potential. Addressing economic inequality requires systemic change and policies that promote equitable distribution of resources and opportunities for all.

Education Disparities

Access to quality education is essential for personal and societal growth, yet many individuals face barriers to accessing educational opportunities. Factors such as socioeconomic status, race, ethnicity, and gender identity can impact access to education and contribute to disparities in academic achievement. Addressing education disparities requires investments in equitable funding, culturally responsive curriculum, and support services that meet the diverse needs of all students.

Healthcare Access

Access to healthcare is a fundamental human right, yet many individuals face barriers to accessing affordable and culturally competent care. Lack of access to healthcare services can prevent individuals from receiving necessary medical treatment, preventive care, and mental health support. Addressing healthcare access requires policies that expand coverage, eliminate discrimination, and promote inclusive healthcare practices that meet the needs of diverse populations.

Systemic Oppression

Systemic oppression refers to the pervasive and ingrained systems of power and privilege that perpetuate inequality and discrimination. These systems, which include racism, sexism, homophobia, transphobia, and ableism, create barriers to growth and opportunity for marginalized communities. Addressing systemic oppression requires dismantling discriminatory policies and practices, amplifying marginalized voices, and centering equity and justice in all aspects of society.

Environmental Justice

Environmental factors can also play a significant role in growth prevention, particularly for communities disproportionately affected by pollution, environmental degradation, and climate change. Environmental injustice exacerbates health disparities, economic inequality, and social inequity, preventing individuals from thriving in their communities. Addressing environmental justice requires policies that prioritize the needs of frontline communities, promote sustainable development, and mitigate the impacts of environmental harm.

Intersectionality And Interconnectedness

It is essential to recognize the interconnected nature of growth prevention and the ways in which different forms of oppression intersect and compound one another. Intersectionality acknowledges that individuals experience multiple forms of oppression simultaneously, and addressing growth prevention requires an intersectional approach that considers the intersecting factors of race, class, gender, sexuality, disability, and other identities.

In the intricate tapestry of society, growth prevention creates barriers that hinder personal, emotional, and societal development. Addressing these barriers requires systemic change, collective action, and a commitment to equity and justice for all. By understanding the mechanisms of growth prevention and working to dismantle oppressive systems, we can create environments where individuals can thrive and reach their full potential, unencumbered by barriers to growth and opportunity.

Overcoming Self-Growth Prevention

In the intricate journey of personal development, individuals often encounter internal barriers that impede their growth and hinder their ability to reach their full potential. These internal obstacles, collectively referred to as self-growth prevention, can manifest in various ways and impact different aspects of life, including self-esteem, relationships, career advancement, and overall well-being. Understanding and addressing self-growth prevention is essential for fostering resilience, promoting self-empowerment, and unlocking the path to personal growth and fulfillment.

Self-Limiting Beliefs

At the heart of self-growth prevention are self-limiting beliefs—negative perceptions and assumptions about oneself, one's abilities, and one's worthiness. These beliefs often stem from past experiences, societal conditioning, and internalized messages of inadequacy or unworthiness. Common self-limiting beliefs include "I'm not good enough," "I don't deserve success," or "I'm destined to fail." Overcoming self-limiting beliefs requires challenging negative thought patterns, practicing self-compassion, and cultivating a growth mindset that acknowledges the potential for change and self-improvement.

Fear Of Failure

Fear of failure is another significant barrier to self-growth, preventing individuals from taking risks, pursuing new opportunities, and stepping outside their comfort zones. This fear is often rooted in a desire to avoid disappointment, rejection, or judgment from others. However, embracing failure as a natural part of the learning process can lead to valuable insights, resilience, and personal growth. Overcoming the fear of failure requires reframing setbacks as opportunities for growth, embracing vulnerability, and cultivating a sense of self-worth that is independent of external validation.

Perfectionism

Perfectionism is a common form of self-growth prevention characterized by an unrealistic pursuit of flawlessness and an intense fear of making mistakes or falling short of high standards. While striving for excellence can be admirable, perfectionism can become paralyzing, leading to procrastination, self-criticism, and burnout. Overcoming perfectionism involves challenging all-or-nothing thinking, setting realistic goals, and practicing self-compassion in the face of setbacks or perceived failures.

Self-Sabotage

Self-sabotage is the act of undermining one's own success or well-being through unconscious behaviors, thoughts, or actions. This can include procrastination, self-doubt, negative self-talk, and engaging in self-destructive behaviors. Self-sabotage often stems from deep-seated feelings of unworthiness, fear of success, or a desire to maintain the status quo. Overcoming self-sabotage requires developing self-awareness, identifying triggers and patterns of behavior, and implementing strategies to counteract self-defeating tendencies.

Lack Of Self-Compassion

A lack of self-compassion is a common barrier to self-growth, characterized by harsh self-criticism, perfectionism, and a tendency to prioritize the needs of others over one's own well-being. Cultivating self-compassion involves treating oneself with kindness, understanding, and acceptance, especially in times of difficulty or failure. By practicing self-compassion, individuals can build resilience, improve self-esteem, and create a foundation for sustainable personal growth and well-being.

Comparison And Social Media Influence

In today's digital age, comparison and the influence of social media can serve as significant barriers to self-growth. Constant exposure to curated images of success and perfection can lead to feelings of inadequacy, envy, and a distorted sense of reality. Overcoming the impact of comparison and social media influence requires cultivating self-awareness, setting boundaries, and focusing on personal growth rather than external validation.

Comfort Zone Confinement

The comfort zone is a familiar and safe space where individuals feel secure and at ease. However, remaining within the comfort zone can prevent personal growth and limit opportunities for learning and development. Stepping outside the comfort zone involves embracing discomfort, taking calculated risks, and challenging oneself to explore new experiences and perspectives.

Lack Of Goal-Setting And Direction

Without clear goals and direction, individuals may feel adrift and uncertain about their path forward. A lack of goal-setting can prevent individuals from taking concrete steps toward personal growth and fulfillment. Setting SMART (Specific, Measurable, Achievable, Relevant, Time-bound) goals provides clarity and direction, allowing individuals to focus their energy and resources on activities that align with their aspirations and values.

Negative Self-Talk And Inner Critic

Negative self-talk and the inner critic can undermine self-confidence, fuel self-doubt, and reinforce self-limiting beliefs. The inner critic is an internal voice that criticizes and judges one's thoughts, actions, and abilities. Overcoming negative self-talk involves challenging irrational beliefs, reframing negative thoughts, and practicing self-compassion and self-affirmation.

Resistance To Change

Change is an inevitable part of life, yet many individuals resist it due to fear of the unknown, uncertainty, or discomfort. Resistance to change can prevent individuals from embracing new opportunities, adapting to challenges, and experiencing personal growth. Overcoming resistance to change involves developing flexibility, openness, and a willingness to embrace uncertainty as a natural part of the growth process.

Procrastination And Avoidance

Procrastination and avoidance are common behaviors that can impede personal growth and delay progress toward goals and aspirations. These behaviors often stem from fear of failure, perfectionism, or feeling overwhelmed. Overcoming procrastination and avoidance involves breaking tasks into smaller, manageable steps, creating accountability systems, and addressing underlying emotional barriers that contribute to procrastination.

Unraveling the layers of self-growth prevention requires self-awareness, introspection, and a willingness to confront internal barriers head-on. By addressing comparison and social media influence, stepping outside the comfort zone, setting clear goals, challenging negative self-talk, embracing change, and overcoming procrastination, individuals can create a pathway to personal growth and fulfillment. Through consistent effort and self-reflection, anyone can break free from self-imposed limitations and unlock their full potential.

Complaining

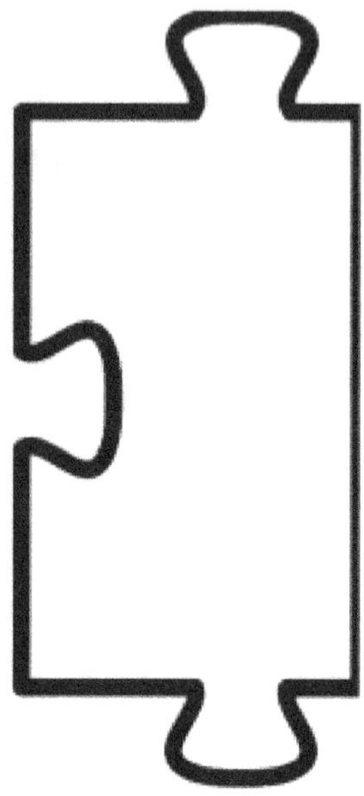

Complaining is a natural human behavior, often stemming from a desire to vent frustrations, seek validation, or express dissatisfaction with a situation. However, when complaining becomes a habitual response without meaningful action, it can have detrimental effects on both individuals and their surrounding environment. By likening complaining to staring at a puzzle piece and insisting it's the wrong shape, we can explore the negative consequences of excessive complaining and the importance of taking proactive steps to address concerns constructively.

Impact On Mental Well-Being

Constant complaining can take a toll on mental well-being, perpetuating a cycle of negativity and discontent. Focusing on problems without seeking solutions can lead to feelings of helplessness, anxiety, and depression. Over time, chronic complaining can erode resilience and optimism, making it more challenging to cope with life's challenges and setbacks.

Strained Relationships

Excessive complaining can strain relationships with friends, family members, and colleagues, creating an atmosphere of negativity and resentment. Constantly venting frustrations without seeking a resolution can alienate others and undermine trust and connection. Over time, individuals may become reluctant to engage with chronic complainers, leading to social isolation and loneliness.

Impact On Productivity And Success

Complaining can also impact productivity and hinder personal and professional success. Constantly focusing on problems can detract from energy and attention that could be better directed toward finding solutions and achieving goals. In the workplace, chronic complainers may be perceived as pessimistic or disengaged, potentially limiting opportunities for advancement and collaboration.

Reinforcement Of Negative Patterns

When complaining becomes a default response to challenges, it reinforces negative patterns of thinking and behavior. Instead of actively seeking solutions or taking proactive steps to address concerns, individuals may become stuck in a cycle of rumination and dissatisfaction. This can perpetuate feelings of victimhood and powerlessness, hindering personal growth and resilience.

Impact On Overall Well-Being

Ultimately, chronic complaining can have a profound impact on overall well-being, contributing to stress, unhappiness, and a diminished sense of fulfillment. By fixating on problems without taking action, individuals may miss out on opportunities for growth, connection, and positive change. Over time, this can lead to a sense of stagnation and disillusionment with life.

Empowerment Through Action

Rather than succumbing to the trap of chronic complaining, individuals have the power to take proactive steps to address concerns and create positive change. This may involve problem-solving, seeking support from others, or reframing challenges as opportunities for growth. By taking action to address concerns constructively, individuals can reclaim a sense of agency and empowerment over their lives.

Erosion Of Positivity

Constant complaining can erode positivity and optimism, creating a negative mindset that colors one's perception of the world. By fixating on problems and frustrations, individuals may overlook opportunities for joy, gratitude, and appreciation. Over time, this negative outlook can become deeply ingrained, making it challenging to find joy and fulfillment in everyday life.

Impact On Physical Health

Chronic complaining can also have a negative impact on physical health, contributing to stress-related ailments such as headaches, muscle tension, and digestive issues. Prolonged stress can weaken the immune system, increase the risk of chronic diseases, and exacerbate existing health conditions. By addressing concerns constructively and adopting healthier coping mechanisms, individuals can reduce the toll that chronic complaining takes on their physical well-being.

Creation Of Toxic Environments

In social and professional settings, chronic complaining can create toxic environments characterized by negativity, conflict, and low morale. Constantly venting frustrations without seeking solutions can poison the atmosphere and undermine teamwork and collaboration. Over time, this toxic dynamic can lead to high turnover rates, decreased productivity, and a culture of resentment and apathy.

Limitation Of Problem-Solving Skills

Excessive complaining can hinder the development of effective problem-solving skills, as individuals become accustomed to dwelling on problems rather than actively seeking solutions. By fixating on the negative aspects of a situation, individuals may overlook opportunities for creative problem-solving and innovation. Over time, this can lead to a sense of stagnation and helplessness, making it difficult to overcome challenges and achieve goals.

Perpetuation Of Victim Mentality

Chronic complaining can perpetuate a victim mentality, where individuals perceive themselves as powerless victims of circumstance. By focusing on external factors and attributing blame to others, individuals may avoid taking responsibility for their own actions and outcomes. Over time, this victim mentality can become deeply ingrained, limiting personal growth and resilience.

Impact On Self-Image

Constantly engaging in negative self-talk and complaining can have a detrimental effect on self-image and self-esteem. By internalizing negative messages and focusing on perceived shortcomings or failures, individuals may develop a distorted view of themselves and their abilities. Over time, this negative self-image can erode confidence and self-worth, making it difficult to pursue goals and aspirations.

Barrier To Growth

Imagine chronic complaining as a roadblock on the path to personal growth. Just like refusing to add new pieces to your puzzle because you're fixated on one that doesn't fit, constant complaints can hinder progress and discourage others from pursuing their own growth journeys. This stagnation impedes individual and collective development, creating a ripple effect of missed opportunities and unfulfilled potential.

Breeding Negativity

The more you complain, the more likely you are to attract like-minded individuals who perpetuate the cycle of negativity. This forms a group dynamic where everyone focuses on the flaws in their respective puzzles, reinforcing pessimism and hindering collaborative problem-solving. Instead of fostering a supportive environment conducive to growth, chronic complaining breeds a culture of negativity that stifles innovation and progress.

Reduced Resilience

Constant complaining weakens your resilience in the face of adversity. It's akin to giving up on a puzzle because you believe it's too difficult rather than exploring alternative strategies for success. This defeatist attitude can spread to others, diminishing the overall resilience of your community and making it harder to navigate life's challenges with determination and optimism.

Damaged Social Capital

Excessive complaining can damage your social standing and inhibit meaningful connections with others. People may begin to avoid your company, viewing interactions with you as draining or unproductive. As a result, your puzzle becomes isolated, depriving you of valuable perspectives and support networks that could help you overcome obstacles and achieve your goals.

Inhibition Of Creativity

Complaining often stifles creative problem-solving by promoting a rigid, closed-minded approach to challenges. Rather than exploring innovative solutions, individuals may become fixated on the perceived shortcomings of their puzzles, limiting their ability to adapt and overcome obstacles. This lack of creativity hampers progress and innovation, leading to a stagnation of growth and development.

Increased Stress Levels

Frequent complaining contributes to heightened stress levels, creating a pervasive sense of unease and discontent. This stress is contagious, spreading throughout your social circle and exacerbating feelings of being overwhelmed and anxious. As stress levels rise, individuals may find it increasingly difficult to focus, make decisions, or find joy in their daily lives, further perpetuating the cycle of negativity.

Loss Of Objectivity

Chronic complaining distorts your perception of reality, making it difficult to assess situations objectively. Like misjudging a puzzle piece based solely on its color, you may overlook potential solutions or opportunities for growth. This loss of objectivity prevents you from seeing the bigger picture and finding creative ways to address challenges, perpetuating a cycle of frustration and discontent.

Creating A Victim Mentality

Persistent complaining fosters a victim mentality, where individuals perceive themselves as powerless victims of circumstance. This passive mindset erodes your sense of agency and control, making it difficult to take proactive steps toward positive change. By attributing blame to external factors rather than taking responsibility for your own actions, you relinquish control over your life puzzle and resign yourself to a sense of helplessness.

Inducing Paralysis By Analysis

Chronic complaining can lead to analysis paralysis, where individuals become overwhelmed by the perceived complexity of their problems. Like staring at a puzzle for so long that you become paralyzed by indecision, excessive complaining can make even simple tasks seem insurmountable. This paralysis inhibits progress and innovation, making it difficult to move forward and find solutions to life's challenges.

Fueling Pessimism

A habit of chronic complaining fosters a pessimistic outlook on life, where challenges are viewed as insurmountable obstacles rather than opportunities for growth. This pervasive sense of pessimism undermines optimism and resilience, making it difficult to maintain motivation and perseverance in the face of adversity. By perpetuating a negative narrative, chronic complaining reinforces feelings of hopelessness and resignation, hindering personal and collective progress.

Undermining Empathy

When you constantly complain without taking action, others may become desensitized to your concerns, reducing the likelihood of empathetic interactions. This lack of empathy diminishes the mutual support essential for personal and collective growth, creating barriers to meaningful connections and collaboration. By fostering a culture of indifference, chronic complaining undermines the sense of community and compassion necessary for navigating life's challenges with resilience and empathy.

Stuck In A Loop

Constant complaining can be like obsessing over a single puzzle piece that won't fit while ignoring the rest of the puzzle. It can trap you in a cycle of negativity, making it hard to see solutions or even other issues that might be easier to tackle.

Influence On Others

Your attitude is catchy, for better or worse. If you're always complaining, it can drag down the mood of those around you. You might notice more people around you also start complaining about their puzzles, making the whole environment less enjoyable.

Mental Toll

Continuous complaining can shape your thought patterns and reinforce a negative mindset. It's like convincing yourself that you'll never finish your puzzle, making it increasingly likely that you won't.

Missed Opportunities

When you're caught up in what's wrong, you might miss what's right—or could be right with a little effort. Complaining can blind you to new puzzle pieces that could be a perfect fit if you just give them a chance.

Strains Relationships

Too much complaining can wear down even the most patient of friends and family. It can become exhausting for them to always be around someone who only sees the missing or ill-fitting pieces instead of the progress made.

Blocks Solutions

If you're too busy complaining, you're not problem-solving. It's hard to find where the next piece goes in your life puzzle if you're not even looking for it.

Lowers Self-Esteem

Over time, constant complaining can eat away at your confidence. This self-doubt makes it even harder to tackle the puzzle of life, creating a cycle that's tough to break.

Erodes Trust

When people notice that you complain a lot but don't take action, they might stop taking your concerns seriously. Your puzzle then becomes something others might avoid, making it difficult to seek or give help when needed.

Loss Of Joy

Constant complaining can sap the fun out of life. Remember, puzzles are supposed to be challenging but also enjoyable. If you're always focused on the flaws, you lose sight of the bigger, beautiful picture you're creating.

It's normal to feel stuck or frustrated sometimes, just like it's normal to struggle with a particularly tricky section of a puzzle. The key is to not let complaining become your go-to response. Instead, use those moments as a signal to pause, assess the situation, and look for practical ways to make progress. By doing this, you not only improve your own puzzle-solving experience but also set a more positive example for those around you.

While it's natural to express concerns or frustrations from time to time, chronic complaining without taking action can have far-reaching negative effects on individuals and their surrounding environment. By recognizing the impact of chronic complaining on positivity, physical health, social dynamics, problem-solving skills, mentality, and self-image, individuals can take proactive steps to address concerns constructively and cultivate a more positive and fulfilling life.

Supporting Others on Their Journey

Guidance For Friends, Family, And Allies On Supporting LGBTQIA+ Individuals.

Let's dig into how friends, family, and allies can be the best support team for LGBTQIA+ folks who are piecing together their own life puzzles. Supporting someone else's journey doesn't mean you know all the answers. Actually, it's the opposite. It's about giving them the space and tools they need to figure out their own puzzle.

Listen Up

This is rule number one for a reason. When someone shares a piece of their puzzle, like coming out or talking about their feelings, it's important to actually listen. Think about it like this - you wouldn't jam a puzzle piece into a spot it doesn't fit, right? Listen without planning what you're going to say next.

Be There

Sometimes, people just need a friend to sit with them while they work on their puzzles. You don't have to solve it for them or even help pick up the pieces. Just your presence can be super comforting.

Respect Their Pace

Some puzzles come together super fast. Others take a lot of time. And that's totally okay. The point is, don't rush them. If they're not ready to talk or share, give them the time they need.

Ask, Don't Assume

If you're not sure what someone needs, it's way better to ask than to guess. Maybe they need a specific puzzle piece, like a term or label, explained. Or maybe they want you to come with them to an LGBTQIA+ event. By asking, you show that you respect their journey as their own.

Educate Yourself

If you're gonna be a good puzzle buddy, you should know what the picture might look like. Please read up on LGBTQIA+ issues, learn the terms, and understand the challenges they face. This helps you be a better ally and makes you more helpful when they do want advice or info.

Keep Their Stuff Private

Sometimes, a puzzle is a personal masterpiece not ready for public viewing. If someone shares something private with you, keep it that way unless they say otherwise. Trust is super important.

Own Your Mistakes

Let's say you accidentally put a puzzle piece in the wrong spot or said something not-so-great. It's all part of learning and growing up. The key is to say sorry, mean it, and learn from it.

Celebrate The Wins

Every puzzle piece that fits is a win, big or small. Maybe they came out to someone else, or maybe they found a label that fits them perfectly. A high-five or a kind word can go a long way.

Open Conversations

This goes beyond just listening. Encourage honest talk by asking open-ended questions like, "How do you feel about that?" or "What was that experience like for you?" It helps them think about their own puzzle pieces and how they fit.

Be Mindful Of Language

Words are powerful, kinda like how one piece can change the whole look of a puzzle. Using inclusive and affirming language shows you care. If you're not sure what terms they prefer, just ask!

Offer Resources

Sometimes, the puzzle's picture isn't clear, and that's when a guide or a blueprint can be super helpful. Share articles, books, or places where they can get support. But don't push. Leave it up to them to decide what's useful.

Encourage Self-Exploration

Every puzzle is different because every person is different. Please encourage them to find out what makes their puzzle unique. That might mean joining LGBTQIA+ groups, reading specific literature, or exploring their feelings more deeply.

Adapt And Change

Just like puzzles can have sections that need reworking, your role as a supporter might need to change, too. Maybe you started as a close confidant, but now they need more space to explore on their own. Being flexible shows true respect for their journey.

Family Matters

If you're family, understand that you have a special role in this puzzle-making. Your support—or lack of it—holds extra weight. Being supportive as a family member means not just acceptance but active advocacy within the family and beyond.

Avoid Stereotypes

Not all puzzles look the same. avoid making assumptions based on stereotypes. They limit how a person sees their own puzzle and can really hurt. Stick to what you know about the individual, not what you think you know about a group.

Take Care Of Yourself

Being a great ally or supporter also means taking care of your own puzzle. You're not much help if you're burnt out or struggling yourself. Self-care is not selfish. it makes you a better supporter.

Practice Intersectionality

People are more than just one puzzle. They may be dealing with challenges related to race, disability, or other factors in addition to their gender identity. Being aware of this makes you an even better ally.

Be A Cheerleader, Not A Coach

Remember, it's not your job to direct or manage their journey. Think of yourself as a cheerleader on the sidelines, offering encouragement and support rather than a coach calling the plays. Remember, their puzzle, their rules, but you can totally be there to help them see how all the pieces fit.

Strategies For Creating Inclusive And Affirming Environments.

Creating an inclusive and affirming environment is a big deal, especially for LGBTQIA+ folks. It's like setting up the puzzle board where all pieces, no matter their shape or color, have a spot to fit. So, how can friends, family, and allies help make this happen?

Use Inclusive Language

Seriously, this one's a game-changer. Instead of using gendered terms like "guys" or "ladies," opt for more inclusive words like "everyone," "folks," or "y'all." It's a small change, but it makes the puzzle board way more welcoming.

Normalize Pronoun Sharing

When you meet someone new or even among friends, make it a habit to share pronouns. It takes the guesswork out of the equation and shows you care about getting everyone's puzzle pieces right.

Challenge Non-Inclusive Behavior

Let's say someone at school or work makes an off-color joke or uses a slur. Speaking up might feel awkward, but it's kinda like removing a puzzle piece that doesn't belong. If it's safe to do call it out.

Accessible Information

Whether it's a school, workplace, or even a family gathering, make sure there's easy-to-find info on LGBTQIA+ resources and policies. It's like giving everyone a glimpse of what the completed puzzle could look like.

Showcase Diversity

Representation matters. Think of posters, art, or guest speakers that reflect different identities. When people see puzzles that look like theirs, they feel more comfortable bringing their own pieces to the table.

Safe Spaces

Create zones where LGBTQIA+ individuals can hang out, talk, and share without judgment. It's like setting up a cozy corner where people can work on their puzzles in peace.

Celebrate Important Dates

Recognizing LGBTQIA+ holidays and milestones, like Pride Month or Transgender Day of Remembrance, adds a layer of validation. It's a moment to say, "Hey, your puzzle pieces are just as important as anyone else's."

Feedback Loop

Keep the conversation going. Ask for feedback on what's working and what isn't. It's like checking in to make sure everyone has the puzzle pieces they need.

Training And Education

Organize or attend workshops that focus on LGBTQIA+ inclusion. The more you know, the better you can make the environment for everyone. Think of it as puzzle-solving 101 for everyone involved.

Real-World Application

Take these strategies beyond just one area. Apply them at home, school, work, and in public places you frequent. It's like spreading the puzzle love so everyone has a place to fit in.

Active Allies

Being an ally is more than just a title. It's about actions. Be the person who stands up for inclusivity, not just in big ways but in daily interactions, too. Allies keep an eye out for missing puzzle pieces and help everyone find where they fit.

Update Policies

If you're in a place where you can influence rules—like at work, school, or community groups—push for policies that protect LGBTQIA+ rights. Make sure some guidelines tackle discrimination or harassment. It's like establishing rules that keep the puzzle table a safe space for all.

Flexibility In Forms And Documents

This might sound small, but it's huge. Forms should include a variety of gender options, not just 'male' and 'female.' Plus, offering a way for individuals to self-identify and respect their unique puzzle.

Counseling And Support Services

Access to emotional support, especially from professionals who are trained in LGBTQIA+ issues, can be a lifeline. Think of these services as special tools designed to help fit tricky puzzle pieces.

Peer Support Groups

Sometimes, talking to others who are sorting their own puzzles can offer unique insights. Facilitating or encouraging peer-led groups provides another layer of understanding and acceptance.

Inclusive Restrooms

Gender-neutral or family restrooms can go a long way in making everyone feel included. It's like saying, "Hey, we have a spot at the table for every kind of puzzle."

Inclusive Media And Literature

Books, movies, and other media in communal spaces should reflect diverse experiences. When you see puzzles like yours in stories, it feels like you belong.

Foster Open Dialogue

Create avenues for open discussion where people can express their concerns or experiences without fear of judgment or backlash. This keeps the puzzle environment fresh and updated according to everyone's needs.

Showcase Achievements

Regularly highlight and celebrate the contributions of LGBTQIA+ individuals in your community, school, or workplace. Recognizing individual puzzle pieces makes the entire picture richer.

Amplify Voices

Use your influence to amplify LGBTQIA+ voices, whether it's sharing social media posts, recommending books by LGBTQIA+ authors, or inviting guest speakers. Every voice adds a unique shape and color to the overall puzzle.

Examine And Evolve

Even after setting up an inclusive environment, there's always room for improvement. Regularly review how things are going and be willing to make changes. It's like reevaluating your puzzle to make sure every new piece still has a place.

By integrating these strategies, you contribute to an environment where every puzzle—no matter how complex or simple—is valued. And remember, the goal isn't to make every puzzle the same. it's to make sure every puzzle is welcomed.

Promoting Love, Acceptance, And Understanding

Promoting love, acceptance, and understanding is like adding the glue that holds the whole puzzle together. Without these things, pieces might scatter or not fit well. Here's how to strengthen that bonding glue in various settings

Be A Role Model

show love and acceptance in your own actions. This sets an example for others. If you're fitting your puzzle pieces with care and respect, it encourages others to do the same.

Share Stories

Whether it's personal stories or tales of people who've made a difference, sharing uplifts everyone. Stories offer a glimpse of different puzzles, making it easier to understand where someone else is coming from.

Active Listening

This one's big. To really understand someone, you have to listen—not just hear them. When you actively listen, you're saying, "Your puzzle is important to me, and I want to see how it comes together."

Ask And Learn

If you're not sure what someone needs in terms of love or acceptance, it's okay to ask. It shows you care enough to get it right, sort of like asking for help when you can't find where a puzzle piece fits.

Validate Feelings

Sometimes, a simple "I hear you" or "That sounds tough" can go a long way. Validation is like finding a puzzle piece that someone's been struggling with and helping them see where it fits.

Encourage And Support

Offer positive reinforcement whenever you can. If someone's doing a great job fitting their puzzle pieces together, let them know. A simple "You're doing great" can mean the world.

Offer A Safe Space

Whether it's a room, a conversation, or a support group, a safe space allows people to be their authentic selves. In this space, everyone knows their puzzle is respected.

Question Prejudices

This is a tough but essential one. If you find yourself or others making judgments or assumptions, challenge them. It's like straightening out a bent puzzle piece so it can fit properly.

Build Community

The more people practice love, acceptance, and understanding, the stronger it becomes. Encourage community events or discussions that promote these values. A community is a collection of puzzles that, when united, create an even bigger, beautiful picture.

Celebrate Differences

This one is key. Every puzzle is unique. each piece varies in shape, size, and color. Celebrating these differences adds depth and richness to the entire puzzle environment.

Teach Empathy

Especially among young people, teaching the ability to understand and share others' feelings can be life-changing. Empathy allows for a deeper connection between different puzzles, even if the pictures they form are worlds apart.

Consistency Is Key

Don't just show love and understanding sporadically. make it a habit. Consistent positive actions give people a sturdy, reliable board where they feel safe placing their puzzle pieces.

Be Inclusive In Leadership

Encourage people from diverse backgrounds, including LGBTQIA+ individuals, to take on leadership roles. When diverse people help guide the community, the puzzle board itself becomes more stable and inclusive.

Open Dialogue With Critics

Sometimes, you'll encounter people who resist creating an inclusive environment. Engage with them respectfully to understand their views. You may not change their mind, but you might smooth out a rough patch on the puzzle board for others.

Facilitate Educational Programs

The more people know, the more accepting they usually become. Consider organizing seminars or workshops that cover topics like LGBTQIA+ history or intersectionality. It's like everyone getting a manual on how to handle puzzle pieces gently.

Implement Restorative Practices

Mistakes happen. pieces get misplaced. Instead of blame, focus on how to repair the damage. Restorative practices offer a way to make the puzzle board whole again after something goes wrong.

Promote Work-Life Balance

Stress and burnout can make it hard for people to show love and understanding. Initiatives like flexible hours or mental health days can help. A relaxed hand is better at fitting puzzle pieces.

Set Boundaries

Love and acceptance don't mean letting people walk all over you. Boundaries let everyone know the rules of the puzzle table, ensuring that no one feels taken advantage of.

Prioritize Mental Well-Being

Sometimes, the struggles are internal. Providing resources for mental health can create a more accepting environment. When people feel balanced, it's easier for them to find where their puzzle pieces fit.

Acknowledge And Celebrate Efforts

It takes work to build an inclusive environment. Recognize and celebrate those who are doing their part. It's like giving a high-five to someone who places a tricky puzzle piece.

Mentorship Programs

Seasoned puzzlers can offer invaluable advice to those new to the table. A mentorship program can provide one-on-one guidance to help everyone find where they fit.

Financial Support

This might not be possible for everyone, but if you can, consider supporting LGBTQIA+ organizations financially. Money can provide the resources needed to keep the puzzle table open to everyone.

Review And Update

Your job isn't done when the puzzle looks complete. New pieces will always come in. Regularly review your inclusivity efforts and update them as needed.

By focusing on these areas, you're not just placing individual puzzle pieces. you're caring for the entire board. And when that board is smooth, sturdy, and well-maintained, everyone's puzzle pieces will fit just as they should.

How Respecting And Knowing Oneself Can Inspire And Guide Others To Do The Same

Respecting and knowing oneself is like carefully sorting through your own puzzle before diving into building the larger picture. When you've got your pieces in order, it not only helps you but can guide others, too. Here's how

Self-Reflection As A Tool

Taking time to understand who you are and what you stand for is crucial. When you reflect, it's like flipping all your puzzle pieces picture-side-up. This clarity can inspire others to pause and do their own soul-searching, setting the foundation for a more meaningful life puzzle.

Setting Boundaries

Knowing yourself helps you understand what you're okay with and what you're not. When you set your boundaries firmly, you give others the courage to do the same. Think of it as building the outer edge of your puzzle so others see it's okay to start there, too.

Leading By Example

When you respect and know yourself, it shines through in your actions. You become an example for others, showing them that they can fit their pieces together in a way that's authentic to them. It's like your puzzle becomes a reference picture on the box that others can look to for guidance.

Sharing Your Journey

Talking about your experiences and what you've learned about yourself can be a powerful teaching tool. Your narrative can act like a puzzle guidebook, offering shortcuts and insights for those still sorting their pieces.

Create A Chain Reaction

When one person starts fitting their puzzle together in a thoughtful, respectful way, it can spark a chain reaction. It's like someone seeing how well your puzzle is coming along and getting motivated to work on their own.

Promote Self-Compassion

Be kind to yourself. mistakes are just opportunities to learn. This self-compassion sends a message to others that it's okay if their puzzle isn't perfect. What matters is the effort and the journey to make it whole.

Increased Tolerance For Diversity

When you know and respect yourself, it's easier to appreciate the differences in others. Your puzzle doesn't have to look like everyone else's, and that's totally fine. This acceptance encourages a more diverse and rich tapestry of life puzzles all around.

Authentic Connections

Genuine respect for yourself often leads to deeper, more meaningful relationships. When you're true to your puzzle, you attract people who appreciate you for who you are, not for the picture they want you to create.

Be A Confidence Booster

Self-knowledge often breeds confidence. When you're sure about where your puzzle pieces go, you're not easily swayed by others. This confidence can be contagious, giving those around you the courage to trust their own instincts.

Be A Resource

Once you've been through the process of knowing and respecting yourself, you can offer invaluable advice. You become that go-to person when someone has a tricky puzzle piece they can't place.

Influence The Environment

Your self-respect will often lead you to advocate for an environment where everyone is respected. Just like you wouldn't want to build a puzzle on a shaky table, you'll work to ensure that the setting is supportive of everyone's self-discovery journey.

Passing The Torch

Last but not least, when you know and respect yourself, you're in a better position to mentor others. Your sorted and well-fitting puzzle can be the inspiration for the next generation to start building theirs.

Emotional Resilience

Understanding and embracing your feelings isn't just for you. it shows others that emotions are not weaknesses. Just like a difficult puzzle can have a rewarding outcome, navigating tough emotions can lead to a more resilient self, inspiring others to tackle their emotional puzzles head-on.

Maintaining Integrity

When you know what you stand for and hold true to it, you provide a framework that others might follow. Your integrity is like showing others that every puzzle piece, no matter how insignificant it seems, is vital for the complete picture.

Communication Skills

Knowing yourself also means knowing how you communicate best. Whether you're a talker, a listener, or a doer, your style sends a message about the validity of different communication methods, making the puzzle-building process more inclusive for everyone involved.

Advocacy

Your self-respect might drive you to stand up for yourself and others, becoming an advocate in your community. This can inspire onlookers to not just fit their own puzzle pieces but also to help others find where their pieces belong.

Normalization Of Self-Care

Taking time for yourself isn't selfish. It's necessary. Your commitment to self-care serves as permission for others to take breaks and assess how their puzzle is coming together without feeling guilty about it.

Financial Responsibility

When you know and respect yourself, you understand the value of being financially prudent. This behavior can rub off on others, showing them that wisely managing resources is like having enough space and light to comfortably work on your puzzle.

Balancing Commitments

Knowing your limits allows you to balance work, relationships, and personal time. Observing your balance can guide others in arranging their puzzles in a way that doesn't overwhelm them.

Demonstrating Accountability

Owning up to your mistakes and learning from them encourages a culture of accountability. It shows that flipping a wrong-facing puzzle piece is part of the process, not a failure.

Conflict Resolution

Understanding yourself often means you're better equipped to understand others, making you effective at resolving conflicts. Your approach serves as a practical model for others dealing with their own puzzle snags and bumps.

Networking

Building authentic relationships when you respect yourself attracts similarly respectful individuals. This enriches not only your puzzle but also the overall puzzle landscape, encouraging others to seek meaningful connections.

Life-Long Learning

Being in tune with yourself often ignites a thirst for continual learning. Your quest for knowledge can become the wind beneath someone else's wings, propelling them to also seek more pieces for their life puzzle.

Humility And Gratitude

Knowing yourself keeps you grounded, reminding you that every puzzle, big or small, intricate or simple, is valuable. This humility and gratitude can encourage others to appreciate their own and others' puzzles without comparison.

By firmly rooting yourself in knowing and respecting who you are, you create a lasting legacy. You're not just another puzzler. you become a guide, a mentor, and a source of inspiration that drives others to explore the complex but rewarding landscape of their own puzzles. In this way, the impact of your self-knowledge doesn't just end with you. it perpetuates a cycle of self-discovery, acceptance, and respect that can last generations.

Recap of key themes and messages

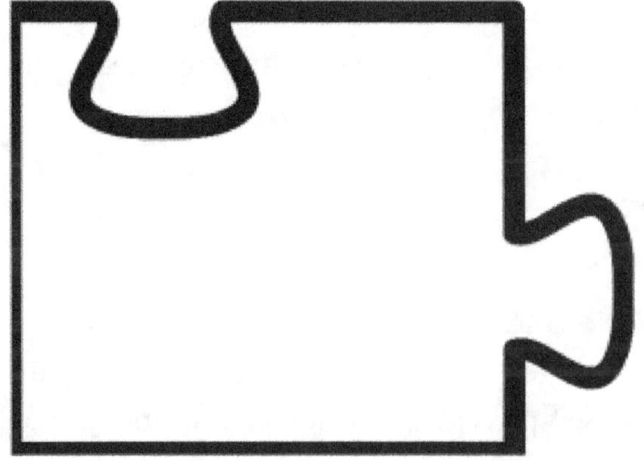

1. Early Years

Laying Down the Edge Pieces

During your early years, you begin to lay down the foundational edge pieces of your life puzzle. These pieces represent the fundamental aspects of your identity and environment, including your family dynamics, cultural background, and formative experiences. The edge pieces provide stability and structure, serving as anchors as you navigate the complexities of growing up.

2. Adolescence

Complicated and Colorful Middle Pieces

As you transition into adolescence, the puzzle pieces become more intricate and colorful. Your gender identity emerges as a significant centerpiece, influencing your self-perception, relationships, and personal development. Understanding and embracing your gender identity can unlock a deeper understanding of yourself and your place in the world, providing a framework for navigating the challenges and opportunities of adolescence with authenticity and confidence.

3. Taking Responsibility For Your Actions

Critical Set of Pieces

Taking responsibility for your actions is a critical set of puzzle pieces that foster personal accountability and growth. These pieces teach you the importance of integrity, empathy, and self-reflection. When you make mistakes or hurt others, these pieces prompt you to acknowledge your errors, make amends, and learn from your experiences. By embracing accountability, you cultivate resilience and integrity, becoming better equipped to navigate life's complexities with grace and maturity.

4. The Lark Code

Cornerstones of Your Puzzle

The LARK Code—Love, Accept, Respect, Know—serves as the cornerstones of your life puzzle, guiding your journey of self-discovery and growth. Loving yourself involves practicing self-compassion and embracing your inherent worthiness, even in the face of challenges or setbacks. Accepting yourself means embracing your unique identity and experiences celebrating your strengths and vulnerabilities alike. Respecting yourself entails setting boundaries, advocating for your needs, and honoring your values and beliefs. Knowing yourself is an ongoing process of self-awareness and introspection, guiding you toward greater authenticity, fulfillment, and alignment with your true essence.

5. Continuous Growth

Your Puzzle is Always Evolving

Your life puzzle is dynamic and ever-evolving, reflecting the ongoing process of growth and self-discovery. With each new experience and milestone, new puzzle pieces emerge, expanding the canvas of your identity and aspirations. Whether it's pursuing further education, embarking on a career path, or forming meaningful relationships, each new chapter adds depth and complexity to your puzzle. Embrace the journey of continuous growth, recognizing that change is inevitable and adaptation is key to navigating life's twists and turns with resilience and grace.

Navigating the puzzle of growing up is a journey of self-discovery, resilience, and evolution. Embrace the complexity of your puzzle, honoring the diverse array of experiences, identities, and aspirations that shape your journey. As you lay down each piece with intention and authenticity, remember to cultivate self-love, embrace accountability, and celebrate your unique essence. Your life puzzle is a masterpiece in the making, reflecting the beauty and complexity of your individuality. Trust in your ability to navigate life's challenges with courage and grace, knowing that every piece contributes to the rich tapestry of your life story.

The Power Of Ongoing Acceptance And Advocacy

Ongoing Acceptance

Think of ongoing acceptance as the specialized tools you use to work on your puzzle, like a puzzle mat or sorting trays. Just as these tools make puzzling easier and more enjoyable, ongoing acceptance ensures that your puzzle remains a fun and meaningful project rather than a stressful chore. As new pieces enter your life—whether it's a new school, relationship, or understanding about yourself—ongoing acceptance allows you to readjust, reshuffle, and rebuild sections as needed. It's about embracing the dynamic nature of your puzzle and being flexible and resilient in the face of change. The more you practice ongoing acceptance, the easier it becomes to integrate new experiences and aspects of your identity into your evolving puzzle.

Advocacy

Imagine you have friends, family, or teachers working on their own puzzles alongside you. Advocacy is like helping them find the right spot for a tricky piece or standing up for them when others try to force a piece where it doesn't belong. It's about recognizing and celebrating the uniqueness of each puzzle, especially within the LGBTQIA+ community where traditional societal norms may not apply. Advocacy creates a space where everyone's puzzle is valued and respected, fostering inclusivity and diversity within the puzzling community.

Contributing To The Puzzling Community

By practicing ongoing acceptance and advocacy, you contribute not only to your own puzzle but also to the larger puzzling community. You set an example of how each unique puzzle is a work of art deserving of acceptance and appreciation. By valuing diversity and embracing individuality, you help create a world where everyone's puzzle is celebrated, regardless of its shape or form. Together, we can build a more inclusive and supportive puzzling community where each puzzle contributes to a richer and more complete picture of humanity.

As you continue to love, accept, respect, and know yourself, remember the importance of ongoing acceptance and advocacy in nurturing your puzzle and supporting others in their puzzling journeys. Your puzzle is an integral part of the larger interconnected web of humanity, each piece contributing to the richness and diversity of the whole. Embrace the dynamic nature of your puzzle, celebrate its uniqueness, and extend a helping hand to those around you. Together, we can create a world where every puzzle is valued and celebrated for its individuality and contribution to the greater picture.

Navigating The Puzzle Of Self-Discovery With The LARK Code

Embarking on the journey of self-discovery and self-love is akin to tackling the world's most intriguing puzzle. The LARK Code—Love, Accept, Respect, Know—serves as your trusted companion, guiding you through the twists and turns of this transformative adventure. Let's explore how each piece of the LARK Code can illuminate your path and empower you on your quest for personal growth and fulfillment.

Love Yourself

When faced with a scattered pile of puzzle pieces, it's natural to feel overwhelmed or discouraged. Loving yourself acts as a beacon of light, illuminating your perspective and reminding you of your inherent worthiness. Each piece of your puzzle, no matter how seemingly insignificant, has a purpose and contributes to the beautiful mosaic of your identity. By showing yourself compassion and kindness, you create a nurturing environment that fosters growth and resilience.

Accept Yourself

There may be puzzle pieces that seem out of place or difficult to reconcile, such as aspects of your identity that others may not understand or accept. Acceptance is the key to embracing every facet of yourself, even those that feel challenging or unconventional. Rather than discarding or denying these pieces, acknowledge their presence and honor their significance in shaping your unique puzzle. Embracing all parts of yourself is essential for achieving wholeness and authenticity.

Respect Yourself

As you piece together your puzzle, you may encounter external pressures or expectations that threaten to disrupt your journey of self-discovery. Respecting yourself means safeguarding your boundaries and asserting your autonomy in the face of societal norms or peer pressure. Your puzzle is yours alone to assemble, and you have the right to determine its composition and design. By prioritizing self-respect, you cultivate a sense of empowerment and agency in shaping your own narrative.

Know Yourself

As your puzzle begins to take shape, you gain insight into your strengths, preferences, and values. Knowing yourself is an ongoing process of self-exploration and introspection, akin to becoming an expert puzzler. By studying your patterns, identifying compatible pieces, and embracing the element of surprise, you deepen your understanding of who you are and what brings you fulfillment. Embracing the evolving nature of your puzzle allows you to approach new experiences with curiosity and confidence, knowing that each addition contributes to your ever-expanding masterpiece.

Your journey of self-discovery and self-love is a dynamic and enriching process akin to assembling a complex puzzle. By embracing the guiding principles of the LARK Code—Love, Accept, Respect, Know—you cultivate a supportive and nurturing environment that fosters personal growth and authenticity. Remember to be patient with yourself, celebrate each milestone, and enjoy the unfolding beauty of your unique puzzle. With the LARK Code as your compass, you navigate the intricacies of self-discovery with courage, resilience, and an unwavering commitment to embracing the masterpiece that is you.

Don't Feel Guilty

A Heavy Burden To Carry

Feeling guilty about who you are can be a heavy burden to carry. Still, it's important to remember that you have nothing to feel guilty about. Here's why

You Are Valid

Your identity, thoughts, feelings, and experiences are all valid and worthy of respect. You have the right to exist authentically and to be true to yourself without feeling guilty about it. Embrace who you are with confidence and pride.

You Are Not Alone

It's common to experience guilt or shame about aspects of ourselves that society may stigmatize or marginalize. However, it's essential to recognize that you are not alone in your experiences. Many people struggle with feelings of guilt or shame related to their identity, but that doesn't make you any less deserving of love and acceptance.

Embrace Self-Compassion

Treat yourself with kindness and compassion, just as you would a friend or loved one. Remind yourself that it's okay to make mistakes, to have flaws, and to be imperfect. Cultivating self-compassion can help you develop a healthier relationship with yourself and alleviate feelings of guilt or shame.

Challenge Internalized Messages

Reflect on where feelings of guilt or shame may be coming from. Are they based on internalized messages from society, family, or other influences? Recognize that these messages are not a reflection of your worth or value as a person. Challenge them with positive affirmations and counterarguments that affirm your identity and self-worth.

Seek Support

If feelings of guilt or shame are overwhelming or persistent, consider seeking support from a therapist, counselor, or support group. Talking to someone who is nonjudgmental and understanding can help you process your feelings and develop coping strategies for managing guilt and shame.

Focus On Self-Acceptance

Practice self-acceptance by embracing all aspects of yourself, including those you may feel guilty about. Remember that you are a complex and multifaceted individual, and it's okay to embrace your unique identity, even if it doesn't align with societal expectations or norms.

Language And Pronouns

Recognizing the difference between biological sex and gender is important for using inclusive language and respecting individuals' pronouns. Using correct pronouns and language that aligns with individuals' gender identities helps create a more welcoming and affirming environment for transgender and gender-diverse individuals.

Cultural And Religious Perspectives

Understanding the distinction between biological sex and gender allows us to appreciate the diversity of cultural and religious perspectives on gender identity and expression. Many cultures and religions have unique understandings of gender that may differ from Western concepts, highlighting the importance of cultural humility and respect for diverse beliefs and practices.

Legal Protections And Rights

Distinguishing between biological sex and gender is necessary for advocating for legal protections and rights for transgender and gender-diverse individuals. This includes advocating for anti-discrimination laws, hate crime protections, and policies that affirm the rights of individuals to access gender-affirming healthcare and participate fully in society.

Self-Acceptance And Self-Love

Embracing who you are, without guilt or shame, is essential for cultivating self-acceptance and self-love. It's about recognizing your inherent worth and value as a unique individual deserving of love, respect, and compassion. When you let go of feelings of guilt, you create space for self-acceptance and empowerment to flourish.

Authenticity And Integrity

Living authentically means being true to yourself and honoring your innermost thoughts, feelings, and desires. When you feel guilty about who you are, you may be tempted to hide or suppress aspects of yourself that you perceive as unacceptable or unworthy. However, embracing your authentic self allows you to live with integrity and honesty, aligning your actions with your true values and beliefs.

Freedom From External Expectations

Letting go of guilt liberates you from the weight of external expectations and judgments. When you stop seeking validation and approval from others and instead focus on honoring your own truth, you reclaim your power and agency. You no longer feel beholden to societal norms or standards that don't align with your authentic self.

Emotional Well-Being And Mental Health

Guilt and shame can take a toll on your emotional well-being and mental health, leading to feelings of anxiety, depression, and low self-esteem. When you release feelings of guilt and embrace self-compassion, you create space for healing and growth. You allow yourself to experience joy, fulfillment, and inner peace, free from the burden of self-condemnation.

Empowerment And Resilience

Embracing who you are, unapologetically and without guilt, is an act of empowerment and resilience. It's about standing tall in your truth, even in the face of adversity or criticism. When you own your identity and value yourself unconditionally, you become a beacon of strength and inspiration for others, empowering them to do the same.

Letting go of feelings of guilt about who you are is essential for cultivating self-acceptance, authenticity, and emotional well-being. It's about embracing your true self with love and compassion, honoring your inherent worth and dignity as a unique individual. When you release feelings of guilt and shame, you open yourself up to a life of freedom, joy, and fulfillment, where you can thrive as your authentic, unapologetic self.

Overall, don't let feelings of guilt or shame hold you back from fully embracing who you are. You deserve to live authentically and unapologetically, free from the weight of self-condemnation. Embrace self-acceptance, cultivate self-compassion, and surround yourself with supportive people who celebrate and affirm your identity. You are worthy of love, respect, and acceptance just as you are.

Resources

The Spectrum's voice

It's fantastic to know that there's a resource like The Spectrum's Voice that aims to provide comprehensive educational support for the LGBTQIA+ community. Here's a breakdown of some of the aspects you can explore on their website

Educational Timeline

This sounds like a valuable resource to understand the history and progress of the LGBTQIA+ community. It's like putting together the pieces of a historical puzzle, tracking important events and milestones.

Awareness Dates

Awareness dates are like markers on the calendar that remind us to celebrate achievements, commemorate struggles, and promote understanding. They're essential for keeping track of the progress made.

Laws And Advocacy

Knowing the laws that protect LGBTQIA+ rights is like having a set of rules for the puzzle game. It helps ensure everyone gets a fair chance and is treated with respect and equality.

Representation And Symbolism

Just as puzzle pieces come in all shapes and colors, different genders and expressions make our world diverse and beautiful. Understanding various representations and symbols is like appreciating the unique pieces in the puzzle of humanity.

Cultural And Mythological Insights

Cultures and myths from around the world are like pieces from different puzzles that come together to create a rich tapestry of stories and identities. Learning about these is like discovering hidden treasures.

Medical Field Changes

It's important to stay updated on the latest developments in the medical field related to gender identity. This knowledge is like getting a new puzzle piece that helps improve understanding and care.

Community Organizations

These organizations are like the glue that holds the puzzle together. They provide support, resources, and a sense of belonging to individuals navigating their gender identities.

Lexicon Of Words

Words are like the language of the puzzle. Understanding and using the right words can help bridge gaps in communication and foster empathy and respect.

Heroes And Trailblazers

Heroes and trailblazers are like the master puzzle solvers who inspire others. Learning about their journeys can motivate and empower individuals within the LGBTQIA+ community.

Your Voice Matters

Just as every puzzle piece matters, so do your thoughts, opinions, and feelings. Sharing your views and experiences can help others feel less alone and more understood.

It's crucial to have resources like The Spectrum's Voice that provide a safe and inclusive space for learning and discussion. Remember, exploring these topics can be like solving a puzzle—sometimes challenging but incredibly rewarding when you see the bigger picture. Your support and engagement with such initiatives can help create a more inclusive and understanding world for everyone.

Resources For Help

Organizations And Businesses That Help The Community

Connecting with organizations and businesses that support the LGBTQIA+ community is like finding the missing pieces of your puzzle. These resources can provide assistance, guidance, and a sense of belonging. Here are some types of resources and organizations you can explore

Lgbtqia+ Support Groups

These are like puzzle clubs where you can meet others who are on similar journeys. They provide a safe space for sharing experiences and finding support.

Mental Health Services

Mental health support is crucial. Organizations that offer counseling and therapy specifically tailored to LGBTQIA+ individuals can be like lifelines during challenging times.

Transgender And Non-Binary Support

For individuals exploring their gender identity, some organizations specialize in providing resources and assistance. They can help with everything from navigating healthcare to legal matters.

Youth And Family Support

For LGBTQIA+ youth and their families, some organizations offer resources and counseling to foster understanding and acceptance.

Healthcare Providers

Finding LGBTQIA+-friendly healthcare providers is important for medical care that respects and understands your unique needs.

Legal Support

Legal organizations can assist with issues like name and gender marker changes, discrimination, and advocacy for LGBTQIA+ rights.

Businesses And Employers

Supporting LGBTQIA+-friendly businesses can create inclusive workplaces. Look for businesses that have diversity and inclusion policies in place.

Allies And Advocacy Groups

Allies play a crucial role in creating a more inclusive world. There are advocacy groups and organizations that work to promote understanding and equality.

Crisis Helplines

Sometimes, life throws tough challenges our way. Crisis helplines, both national and local, can be a lifeline during difficult moments.

Community Centers

LGBTQIA+ community centers are like social hubs where you can find resources, events, and a sense of belonging.

Online Resources

Don't forget about the power of the internet. Many websites and online forums offer information and support for LGBTQIA+ individuals.

Educational Institutions

Some schools and universities have LGBTQIA+ resource centers that provide support for students, staff, and faculty.

Local Lgbtqia+ Events

Attending local LGBTQIA+ events and Pride celebrations can help you connect with your community and discover resources and organizations in your area.

Online Resources

Websites like GLSEN (Gay, Lesbian, & Straight Education Network) provide educational resources for LGBTQIA+ students and educators. Online forums like Reddit's r/lgbt offer a platform for community discussion and support.

Educational Institutions

Some universities, such as the University of California, Berkeley, have LGBTQIA+ resource centers that provide services and support for students and faculty.

Exploring these resources can be like navigating a rich and diverse landscape, each offering unique support and assistance. Remember that you don't have to go through this journey alone. there are many individuals and organizations dedicated to helping you find your place in the LGBTQIA+ community and beyond.

Leveraging Resources In Your Gender Identity Journey

Resources play a pivotal role in navigating the intricate puzzle of understanding your gender identity. They act as the guiding tools that help you piece together the puzzle pieces and create a clearer picture of who you are. Let's delve deeper into the various types of resources and how they contribute to your journey of self-discovery.

Educational Resources

Think of educational resources as puzzle instructions that provide clarity and guidance. These can include books, articles, websites, and educational videos that offer valuable insights into different aspects of gender identity. Whether exploring biological, psychological, or social factors, these resources equip you with the knowledge and understanding necessary to navigate your identity journey with confidence and clarity.

Support Resources

Support resources serve as the comforting puzzle pieces that fit together seamlessly, offering a sense of community and understanding. LGBTQIA+

organizations, support groups, and hotlines provide invaluable support and guidance when you're feeling overwhelmed or in need of connection. Much like a trusted friend who assists you in finding the right spot for a puzzle piece, these resources offer empathy, validation, and a sense of belonging as you navigate your journey.

Personal Resources

Personal resources are the specialized tools you use to work on your puzzle, such as inner strength, self-reflection, and the support of loved ones. These resources empower you to explore and embrace your gender identity authentically. They serve as the foundation upon which you build resilience and self-confidence, guiding you through moments of uncertainty and self-discovery with grace and courage.

Professional Resources

Professional resources act as the puzzle experts who provide expert guidance and support. Therapists, counselors, and medical professionals specializing in gender-related issues offer invaluable insights and strategies to navigate the complexities of your identity journey. Their expertise and support serve as a beacon of guidance, helping you overcome obstacles and achieve greater clarity and understanding along the way.

By leveraging these diverse resources, you enhance your ability to navigate the puzzle of your gender identity with confidence and resilience. They provide the essential tools and support necessary to find the right pieces, put them together, and create a beautiful and complete picture of who you are. As you embark on this journey of self-discovery, remember that you are not alone. There are resources available to support and empower you every step of the way. Embrace them as your trusted puzzle-solving tools, and let them illuminate your path toward authenticity and fulfillment.

Cultivating Gratitude in the LGBTQIA+ Journey

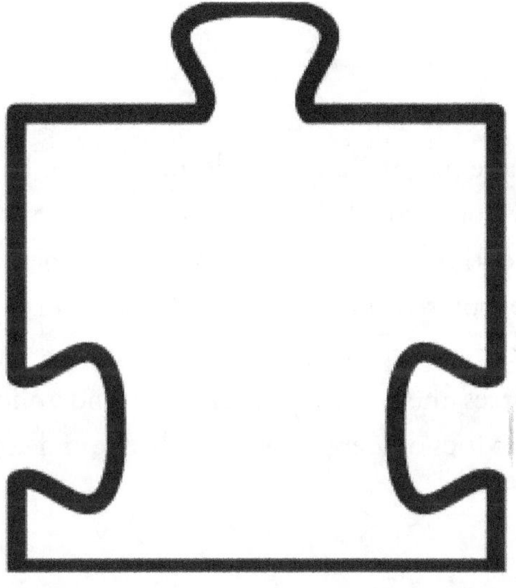

Cultivating Gratitude in the LGBTQIA+ Journey

In the LGBTQIA+ journey, showing gratitude to those who have contributed, much like thanking people for helping you solve a challenging puzzle, is essential for fostering a sense of connection, appreciation, and belonging. Let's delve deeper into the different aspects of gratitude and how they shape and enrich the LGBTQIA+ experience.

Individuals

Individuals in your life are akin to the puzzle pieces that make up your personal support system. These may include friends, family members, mentors, or allies who have stood by you, provided emotional support, and encouraged you to embrace your authentic self. Expressing gratitude to these individuals involves acknowledging their presence and impact on your journey. Whether through heartfelt conversations, gestures of kindness, or acts of reciprocity, saying "thank you" reinforces the bonds of friendship and solidarity that help you navigate the complexities of identity with resilience and courage.

Communities

LGBTQIA+ communities serve as the puzzle board where you fit in, offering a sense of belonging, understanding, and solidarity. Whether it's a local LGBTQIA+ group, an online forum, or a supportive network of peers, these communities provide a safe space for self-expression, validation, and mutual support. Showing gratitude to these communities involves actively participating, lending a listening ear, and contributing to the collective well-being. By fostering a culture of inclusivity, acceptance, and empowerment, you demonstrate appreciation for the sense of belonging and camaraderie they provide.

Organizations

Organizations and advocates within the LGBTQIA+ community act as puzzle makers, creating resources, raising awareness, and advocating for social change. Authors, activists, educators, and nonprofit organizations work tirelessly to promote LGBTQIA+ visibility, understanding, and acceptance. Expressing gratitude to these entities involves amplifying their voices, supporting their initiatives, and advocating for their causes. By acknowledging their contributions, you affirm the importance of their work in fostering greater understanding and acceptance of diverse gender identities and expressions.

Gratitude is a cornerstone of the LGBTQIA+ journey, reflecting appreciation for the support, understanding, and advocacy that contribute to individual and collective empowerment. By expressing gratitude to individuals, communities, and organizations, you honor the interconnectedness of the LGBTQIA+ experience and reaffirm the value of each contribution to the larger puzzle of identity and belonging. Remember that gratitude is not just about saying "thanks" but about recognizing and celebrating the transformative impact of mutual support, solidarity, and allyship in navigating the complexities of gender identity and expression.

Final Words Of Encouragement And Hope

As you navigate your LGBTQIA+ journey, it's essential to recognize the significance of every piece of your puzzle. These final words of encouragement and hope serve as the finishing touch, reminding you of the profound impact of the LARK Code in fostering a more accepting and inclusive world.

Love Yourself

At the core of your journey lies the foundation of self-love. Embracing your gender identity with compassion and acceptance is like discovering the cornerstone of your puzzle. By acknowledging your inherent worthiness and value, you radiate positivity and self-assurance to those around you.

Accept Yourself

Finding the edges of your puzzle signifies the importance of self-acceptance. Your gender identity is valid and authentic, deserving of recognition and respect. Through self-acceptance, you embark on a journey of self-discovery and authenticity, paving the way for personal growth and empowerment.

Respect Yourself

As you navigate the intricate patterns of your puzzle, remember the importance of self-respect. Setting boundaries and demanding dignity and respect from others are integral aspects of honoring your identity. By advocating for yourself, you cultivate a culture of mutual respect and understanding in your community.

Know Yourself

Placing the final piece of your puzzle represents the culmination of self-awareness and authenticity. Knowing yourself entails being attuned to your thoughts, emotions, and desires, fostering a deep sense of confidence and inner strength. Through self-knowledge, you navigate life's complexities with resilience and purpose.

Contributing To A Better World

Living by the principles of the LARK Code extends beyond personal growth. It encompasses a collective commitment to building a more inclusive and compassionate world. Your journey serves as a beacon of hope, inspiring others to embrace their identities and advocate for acceptance and understanding. By embodying love, acceptance, respect, and self-awareness, you contribute to a broader movement toward equality and justice for all.

In these final words of encouragement and hope, remember the profound impact of your journey and the LARK Code in shaping a brighter future. As you continue to embrace your authenticity and celebrate your uniqueness, know that you are an essential piece of the mosaic of human diversity, contributing to a world where every puzzle is valued and celebrated. Keep moving forward with confidence and pride, for your journey is not just about solving your own puzzle but about creating a more accepting and inclusive world for generations to come.

The Spectrum's Voice

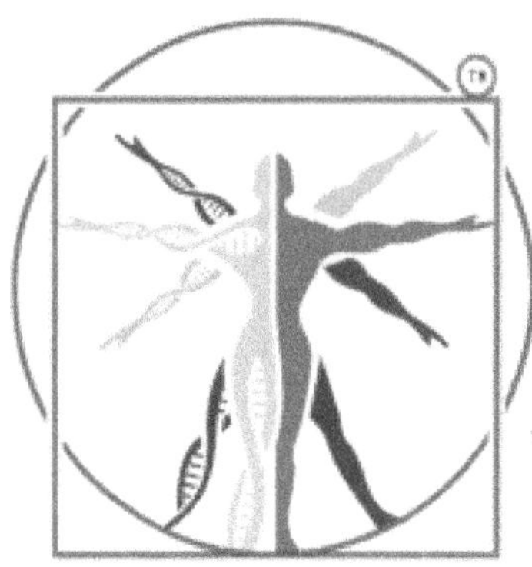

Our Mission

Our mission is to create a safe, inclusive, and supportive digital space that empowers individuals to embrace their true selves, connect with like-minded people, and access essential resources to lead fulfilling lives.

Sharing our stories is like finding puzzle pieces that fit together to create a beautiful picture of understanding and connection.

By opening up and sharing our unique experiences, we're not just telling stories but adding valuable pieces to the puzzle of empathy and unity. These individual pieces, when combined, form a larger, more comprehensive image of our shared human experience. When you share your story, you're contributing a piece to the puzzle and helping others see the complete, interconnected picture.

www.thespectrumsvice.com

Don't miss out!

Visit the website below and you can sign up to receive emails whenever AF Junior publishes a new book. There's no charge and no obligation.

https://books2read.com/r/B-A-NVLCB-AKZBD

BOOKS 2 READ

Connecting independent readers to independent writers.

Did you love *You Are The Gender You Are - Understanding Gender Identity*?
Then you should read *They Are The Gender They Are - Understanding your
loved one's gender.*[1] by AF Junior!

"They Are the Gender They Are! Understanding the Puzzle of Gender Identity"
is a thought-provoking exploration of the intricate and deeply personal
dimension of human experience known as gender identity. In this enlightening
book, the author, drawing from their own experiences as an LGBTQIA+
individual, skillfully navigates the complexities of gender identity, likening it to
a multifaceted puzzle waiting to be solved.

Through the lens of the author's perspective as an LGBTQIA+ man,
readers are guided through a journey of discovery, much like leveling up their
puzzle-solving skills. With a writing style tailored to all readers, the author
sheds light on the diversity of gender identities, encouraging readers to embrace
a continuous learning process and an unwavering openness to the myriad of
experiences and perspectives that exist within this realm.

---

1. https://books2read.com/u/471YOA

2. https://books2read.com/u/471YOA

The heart of the book emphasizes the crucial importance of empathy, respect, and unwavering support in effectively navigating the intricate puzzle of gender identity. It advocates for a society where individuals of all gender identities can freely and authentically express themselves, breaking free from societal constraints and expectations.

As the book draws to a close, it delivers a powerful call to action. Readers are encouraged to embark on a lifelong journey of education, advocacy, and commitment to building a world that is truly inclusive and understanding of all gender identities. "They Are the Gender They Are!" challenges us to collectively work towards a future where the puzzle of gender identity is not just understood but celebrated, creating a brighter and more inclusive world for all.

Read more at https://www.makingamericagreataltogether.us/california/santa-monica/member/af-junior.

Also by AF Junior

Making America Great Altogether!
Trump's Vision of Maga
Making America Great Altogether - Call to Action

The Spectrum's Voice
The Gender Spectrum
You Are The Gender You Are - Understanding Gender Identity
They Are The Gender They Are - Understanding your loved one's gender.

Watch for more at https://www.makingamericagreataltogether.us/california/
santa-monica/member/af-junior.

About the Author

AF Junior, a dedicated advocate for progress and equality, has spent all his 50 years living in the United States. Growing up in a nation filled with promise and potential, he has witnessed firsthand the challenges and injustices that persist within American society.

From an early age, Junior experienced discrimination in various forms, whether based on race, religion, or socioeconomic status. Despite these obstacles, he remained determined to pursue his dreams and make a positive impact on his community.

Throughout his life, Junior has observed the gradual decline of education standards, seeing how access to quality education has dwindled to less than the basics for many young Americans. He has also witnessed the troubling resurgence of archaic religious beliefs infiltrating secular laws, threatening the principles of separation of church and state that are foundational to American democracy.

As Junior has grown older, he has watched with dismay as politicians exploit and scapegoat marginalized communities, particularly the Spectrum Community, for political gain at each election cycle. This pattern of divisiveness and fear-mongering has only deepened his resolve to advocate for change and unity.

In response to these challenges, Junior has taken action by creating the Making America Great Altogether! website and book series. Through these platforms, he aims to amplify voices like his own and provide a space for constructive dialogue on pressing issues facing the nation.

In addition to raising awareness, Junior is committed to planting seeds of change within the government and the way America should governed. He advocates for implementing qualifications and term limits for candidacy service, believing that such measures can help ensure accountability, integrity, and representation within the political system.

Junior's tireless efforts reflect his unwavering commitment to making America a more just, equitable, and inclusive society for all its citizens. With his passion, determination, and vision for a better future, he continues to inspire others to join him in the journey toward making America great altogether.

Read more at https://www.makingamericagreataltogether.us/california/santa-monica/member/af-junior.

About the Publisher

"Spectrum Publishing is a beacon of inclusivity, dedicated to shedding light on the diverse spectrum of human experiences. Specializing in books that explore the multifaceted dimensions of the LGBTQIA+ community and tackle pressing societal issues, Spectrum Publishing stands at the forefront of advocating for understanding, acceptance, and progress. With titles like 'Making America Great Altogether!' at its core, Spectrum Publishing invites readers on a journey of enlightenment, encouraging dialogue, empathy, and unity."